CW01190120

Wainwright

ADDRESS BOOK

FRANCES LINCOLN

Frances Lincoln Limited
4 Torriano Mews
Torriano Avenue
London NW5 2RZ
www.franceslincoln.com

A. Wainwright Address Book
Copyright © Frances Lincoln Limited 2005

Text and illustrations copyright © The Estate of A. Wainwright 1969, 1970, 1971, 1972, 1973, 1974, 1976, 1977, 1978, 1982 and 1983

All rights reserved. No part of this publication may be reproduced, stored in a retrieval system or transmitted, in any form or by any means, electronic, mechanical, photocopying, recording or otherwise, without either prior permission in writing from the publishers or a licence permitting restricted copying. In the United Kingdom such licences are issued by the Copyright Licensing Agency, 90 Tottenham Court Road, London W1T 4LP.

British Library cataloguing-in-publication data
A catalogue record for this book is available from the British Library

ISBN 0-7112-2514-1

Printed in China
First Frances Lincoln edition 2005

ILLUSTRATIONS

The drawings illustrating this address book come from the sketchbooks of A. Wainwright. The reference number for each sketch follows the title of the sketchbook.

FRONT COVER: ULLSWATER AND GRISEDALE
(*A Third Lakeland Sketchbook* 163)

BACK COVER: KIRKSTILE, LOWESWATER
(*A Second Lakeland Sketchbook* 102)

TITLE PAGE: THE ROAD TO SEATHWAITE
(*A Fifth Lakeland Sketchbook* 387)
Who does not know the road to Seathwaite and who has not thrilled as the view of mountains opens up ahead on a bright morning? This is the supreme way to the supreme hills, and although many walkers now travel the road by car, its morning mist is reserved for those on eager foot.

RIGHT: BIRKS BRIDGE, DUDDON VALLEY
(*A Lakeland Sketchbook* 42)
Birks Bridge carries a simple farm road over the River Duddon but at a rocky gorge so spectacular that it has won lasting renown as a beauty spot *par excellence*. The bridge continues to serve as an inspiration to artists and photographers.

p.4	*A Lakeland Sketchbook* 50
A	*A Fifth Lakeland Sketchbook* 375
	A Second Dales Sketchbook 85
B	*A Lakeland Sketchbook* 57
C	*A Third Lakeland Sketchbook* 226
	A Third Lakeland Sketchbook 179
D	*A Third Lakeland Sketchbook* 231
	A Second Dales Sketchbook 147
E	*Scottish Mountain Drawings Vol. 1* 19
	A Second Lakeland Sketchbook 101
F	*A Lakeland Sketchbook* 35
	A Lakeland Sketchbook 24
G	*A Fifth Lakeland Sketchbook* 385
	A Second Dales Sketchbook 135
H	*Scottish Mountain Drawings Vol. 1* 58
	A Fifth Lakeland Sketchbook 364
I	*A South Wales Sketchbook* 19
	A Fourth Lakeland Sketchbook 298
J	*A Second Dales Sketchbook* 99
	A Third Lakeland Sketchbook 200
K	*A Fourth Lakeland Sketchbook* 241
	A Lakeland Sketchbook 30
L	*A Third Lakeland Sketchbook* 234
	A Fifth Lakeland Sketchbook 335
M	*A Lakeland Sketchbook* 40
	A Lakeland Sketchbook 54
N	*A South Wales Sketchbook* 45
	A Third Lakeland Sketchbook 163
O	*A Dales Sketchbook* 31
	A Fourth Lakeland Sketchbook 317
PQ	*A North Wales Sketchbook* 57
	A Fifth Lakeland Sketchbook 344
R	*A Third Lakeland Sketchbook* 215
	Scottish Mountain Drawings Vol. 1 2
S	*A Lakeland Sketchbook* 73
	A Fifth Lakeland Sketchbook 349
T	*A Fourth Lakeland Sketchbook* 307
	Scottish Mountain Drawings Vol. 1 13
UV	*Scottish Mountain Drawings Vol. 1* 47
	A North Wales Sketchbook 27
W	*Scottish Mountain Drawings Vol. 3* 152
	A Lakeland Sketchbook 6
XYZ	*A Second Lakeland Sketchbook* 160

INTRODUCTION

The exquisite ink drawings in this address book come from the sketchbooks of A. Wainwright, artist, fellwalker and author of the Pictorial Guides to the Lakeland Fells – surely the most original and popular walking guides ever written.

Born in Blackburn in 1907, Alfred Wainwright left school at thirteen to work in the Borough Engineer's office. A holiday to the Lake District at the age of twenty-three kindled a lifelong passion for the fells. Looking back to that visit, he wrote, 'I . . . beheld, from Orrest Head, a scene of great loveliness, a fascinating paradise, Lakeland's mountains and trees and water. That was the first time I had looked upon beauty, or imagined it, even.'

In 1941, Wainwright moved to Kendal, and immediately devoted every spare minute he had to walking the fells which, in due course, turned into research for his first seven Pictorial Guides.

In 1969, *A Lakeland Sketchbook* was published. In typically forthright language, he called it his private rebellion against 'acceptance as art of poverty-stricken and barren inspiration and rank bad execution'. He went on to publish a further twenty-eight volumes of sketches of the landscapes of England, Scotland and Wales. This address book can show only a small selection of his work, but the first five Lakeland Sketchbooks were republished in 2004 and the remaining volumes will be reissued gradually over the coming years. The captions accompanying the sketches in this address book are based on those Wainwright originally wrote. Details of the sketchbooks from which the illustrations are reproduced can be found opposite.

In 1974, Wainwright became Chairman of Animal Rescue, Cumbria, and, thanks to the book royalties he contributed to the charity, a permanent animal shelter was set up near Kendal. He died in 1991 at the age of eighty-four.

USEFUL ADDRESSES AND TELEPHONE NUMBERS

BOARDALE
Cartographers prefer to name this valley Boredale or Bore Dale (while inconsistently conceding that the head of it is Boardale Hause) but writers spell the name Boardale, which seems likelier in the company of so many Grisedales. Nowadays there are no wild pigs, but the valley and its environs on the eastern side of Ullswater are even more enchanting without them, a peaceful backwater of beauty that does not advertise itself, nor needs to.

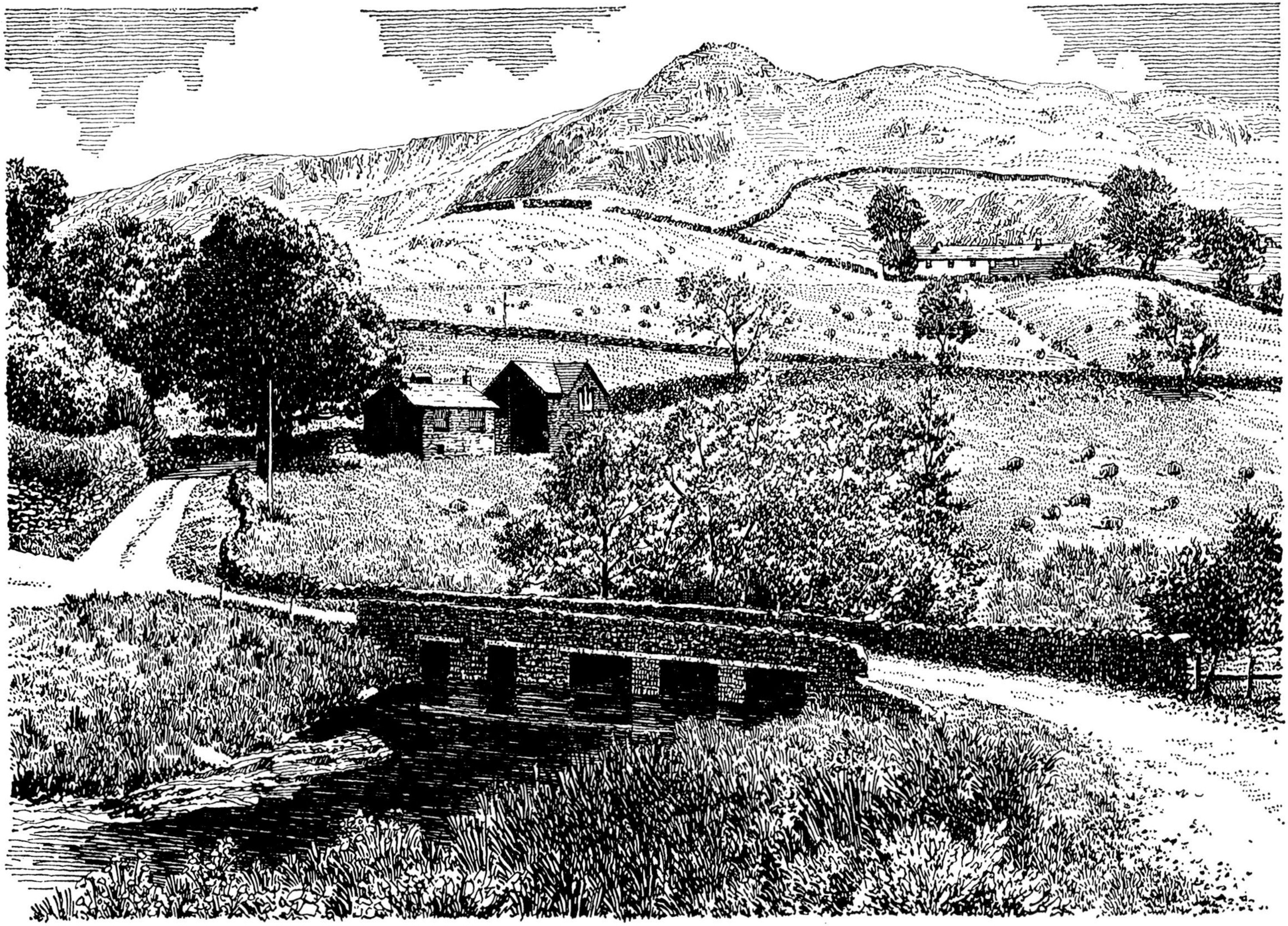

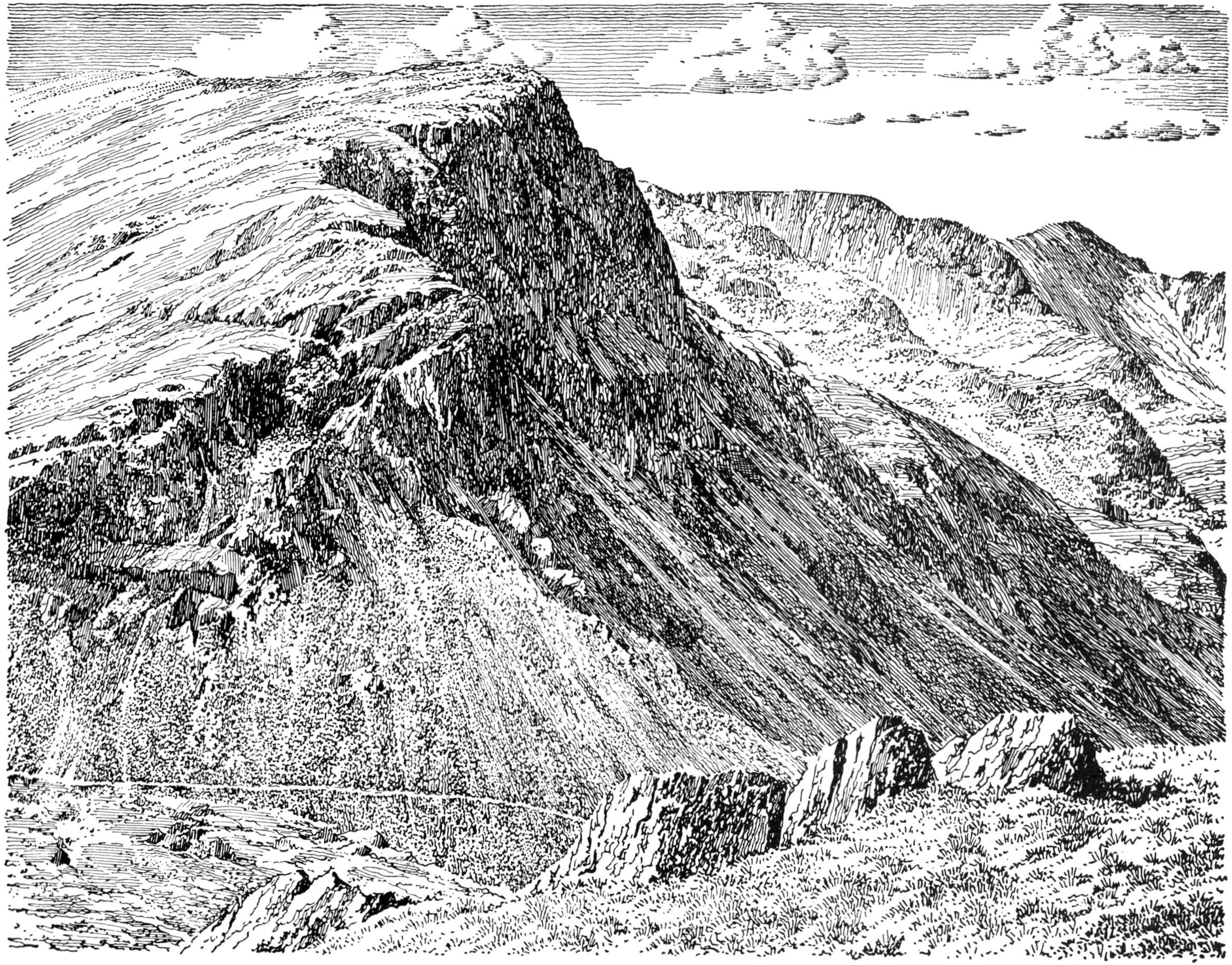

GRISEDALE PASS

A

BULLPOT FARM
The lonely, once-deserted farm of Bullpot, high on Casterton Fell, lost its atmosphere of isolation by the discovery nearby of Lancaster Hole and the Easegill Caverns – the most complex and extensive cave system in the country, with several miles of underground passages.

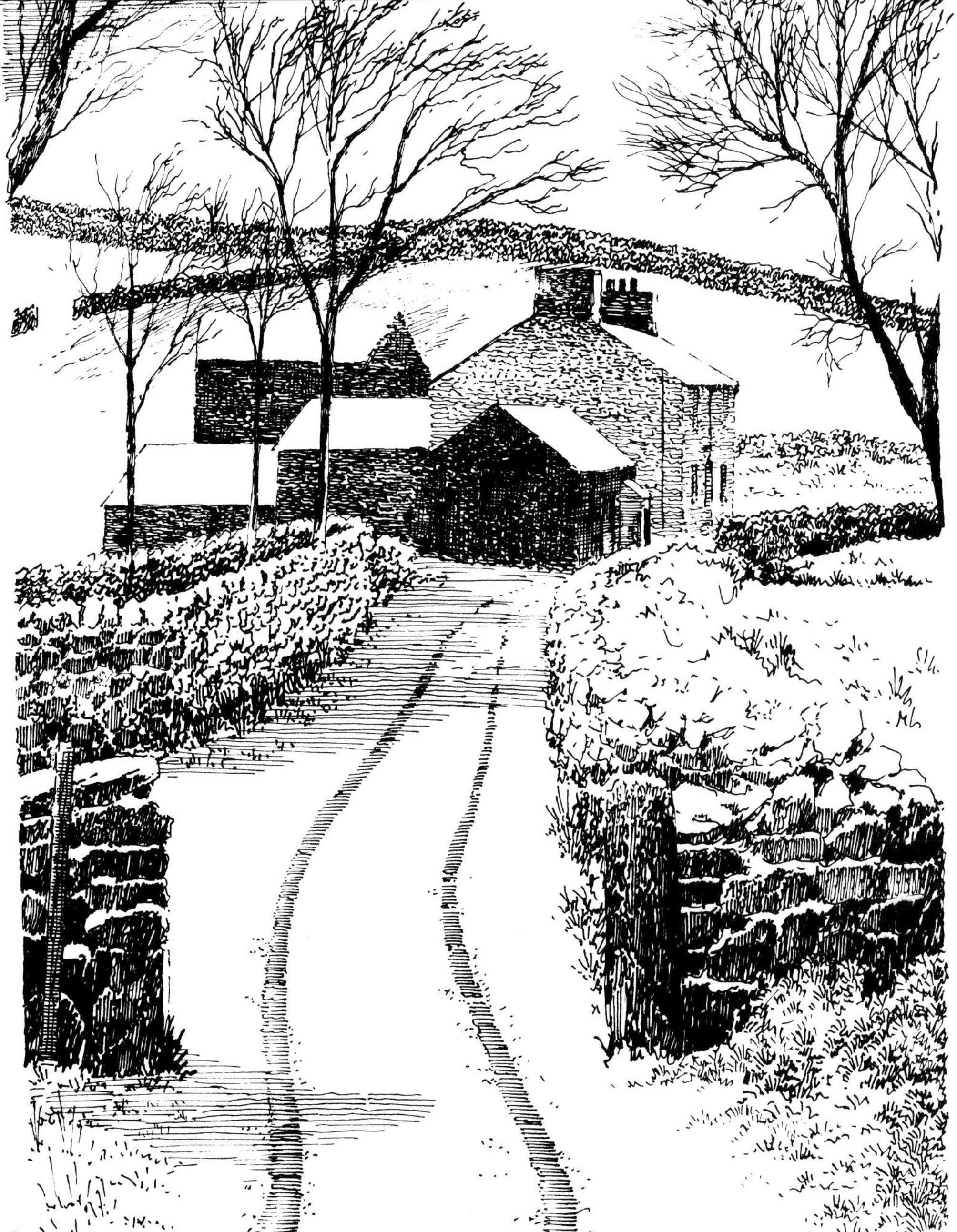

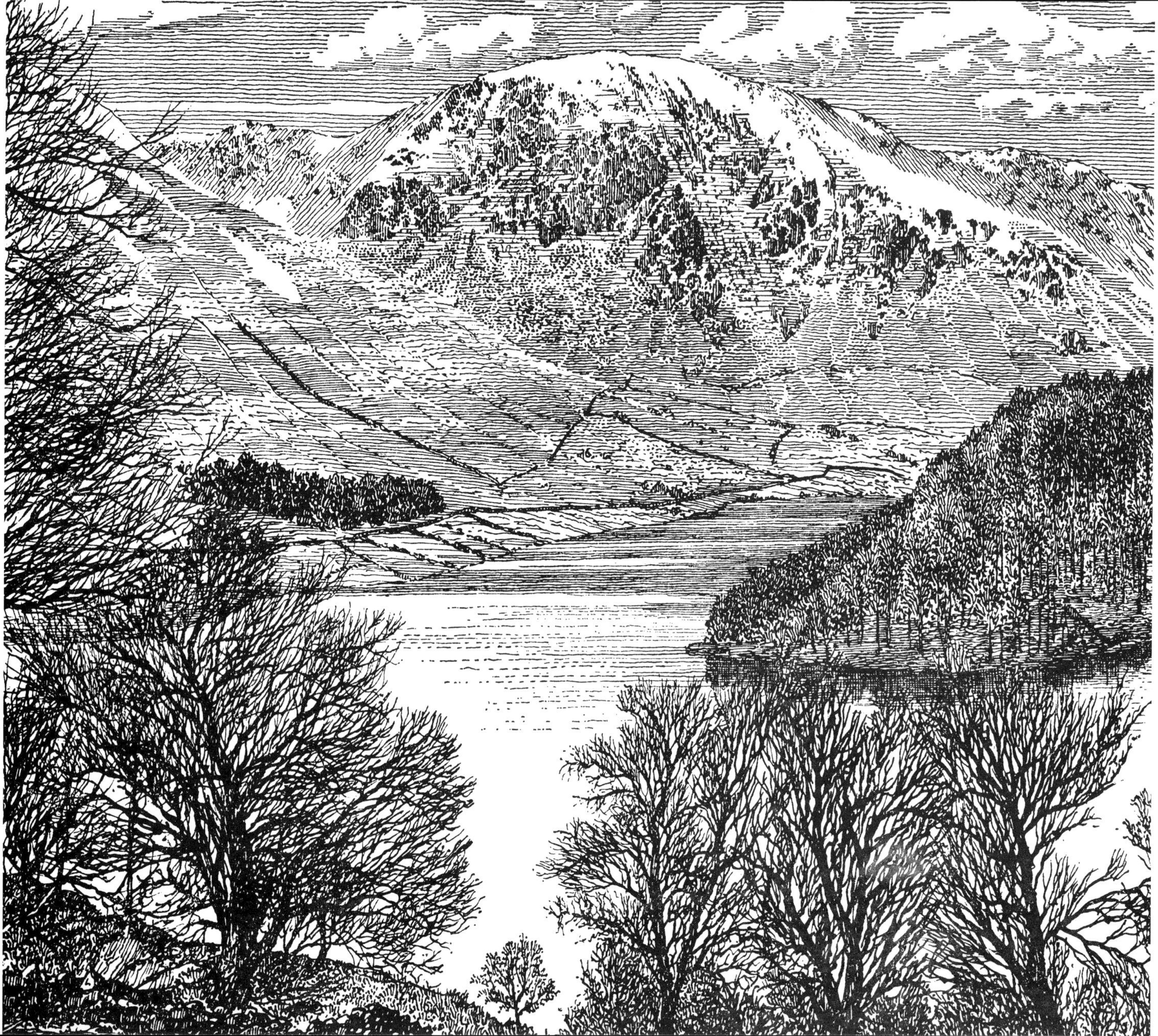

B

HARTER FELL, MARDALE

B

B

B

GRANGE IN BORROWDALE
Grange in Borrowdale presents an animated scene on any summer day, the River Derwent here being very accommodating to holiday visitors, providing picnic places, deep pools for the swimmer and shallow inlets for the paddler in the vicinity of the double bridge, while the little cluster of houses, old mingling with new, caters adequately for more material needs. Even more attractive is the winter scene when the encircling fells lie deep in snow.

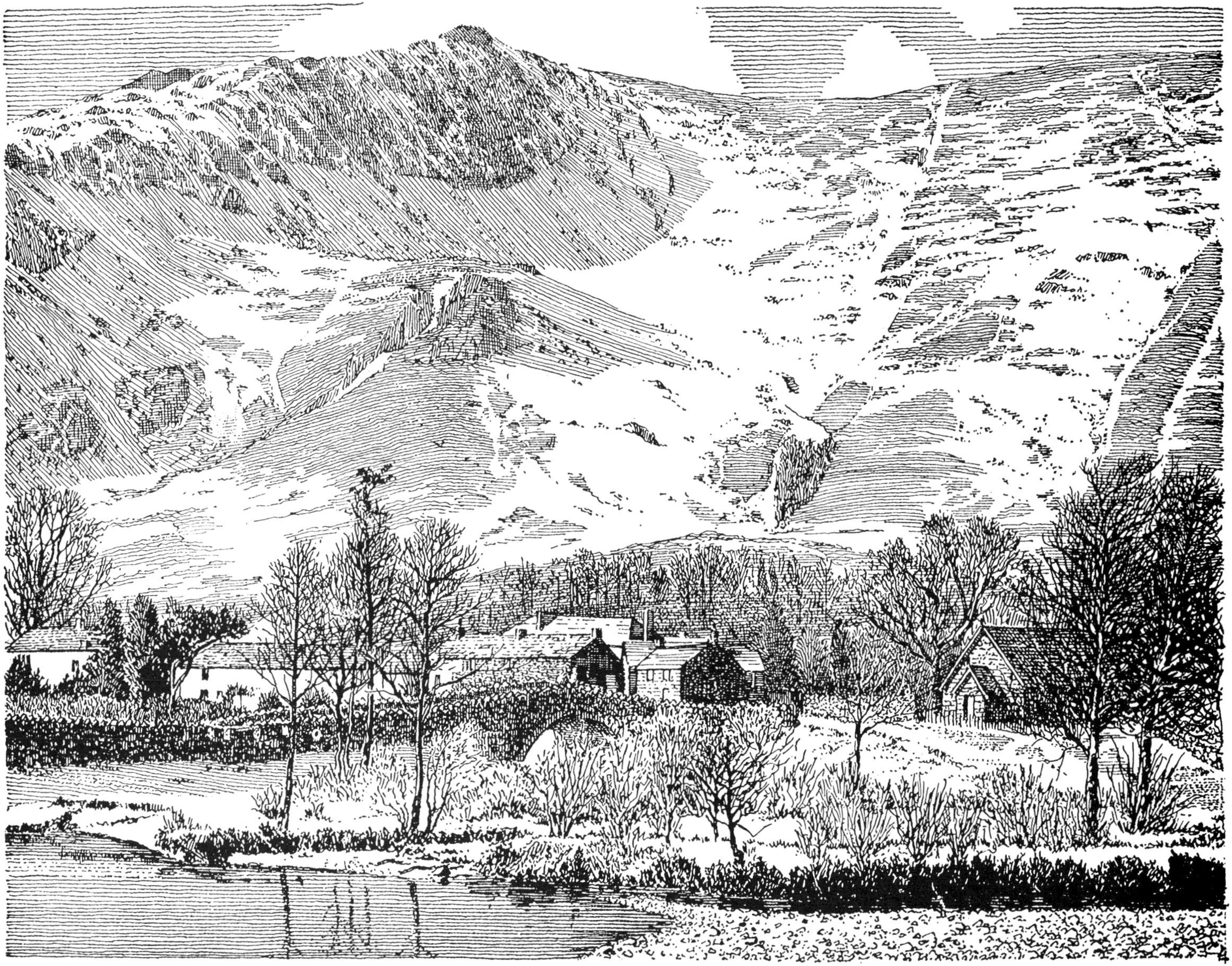

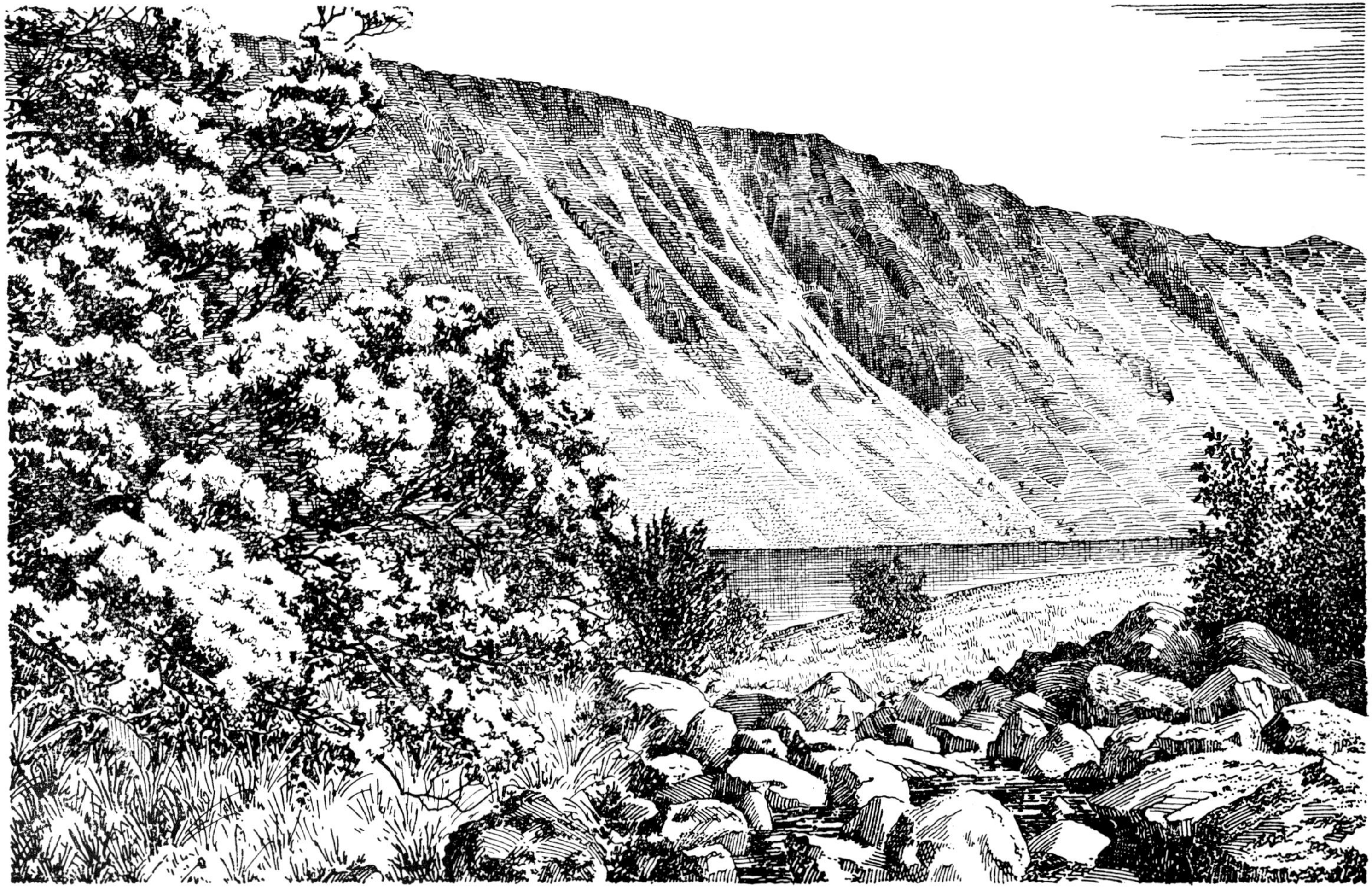

C

WASTWATER
You either love Wastwater or are repelled by it. This deepest and most sinister of the lakes can be both frightening and beautiful. It is a black pit in storm, but arrayed in bewitching colours when the dying sun lights its shattered cliffs and screes.

C

C

C

HIGH CRAG, FROM HAYSTACKS

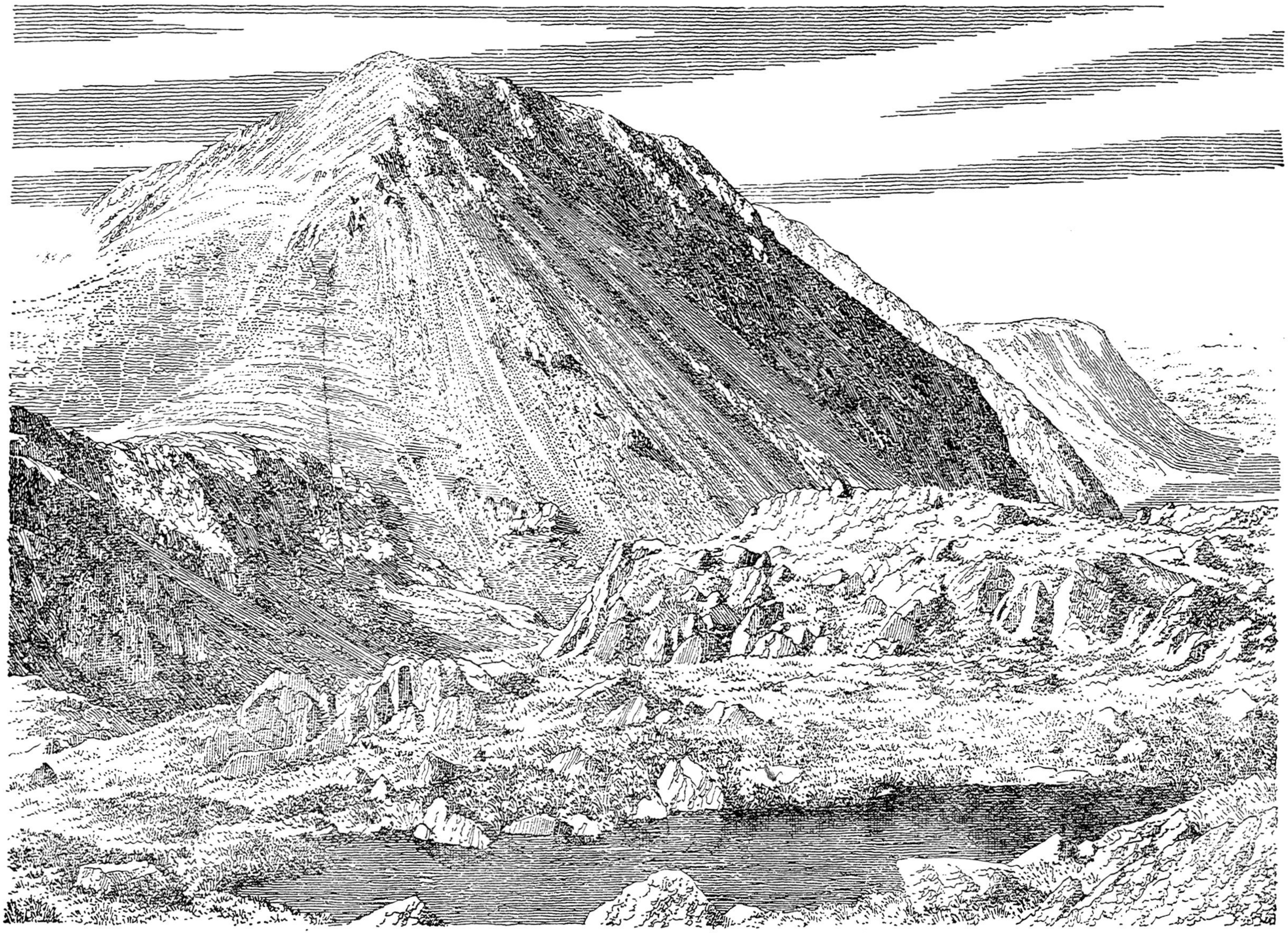

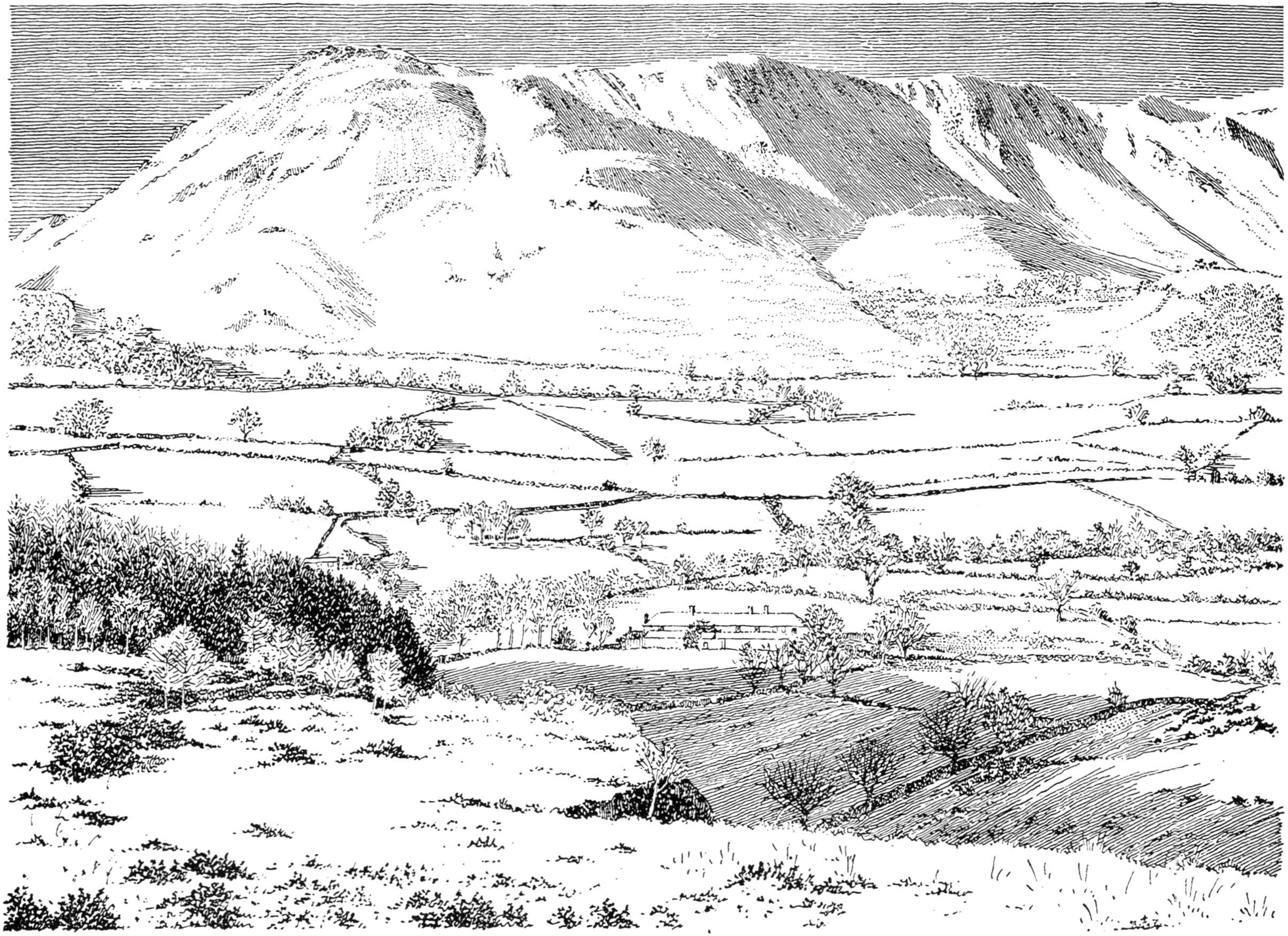

D

LOW FELL, FROM LANTHWAITE HILL
Snow has a remarkable aptitude for greatly increasing the altitude of the fells, or seeming to. Low Fell near Loweswater hardly gets a second glance in summer, but in winter, under new snow, it can look Alpine.

D

D

D

THE CALDER VALLEY
Road, railway, river and canal jostle for space along the narrow floor of the Calder Valley between Todmorden and Hebden Bridge, and mills and cottages add to the congestion, there being little left to please the eye. Before industry took over, however, the valley was green and threaded only by a clear river and a country lane, and the view of it from the high ground adjoining must have been quite lovely. It is still possible, from vantage points on either side, to imagine the rural scene that has since been destroyed.

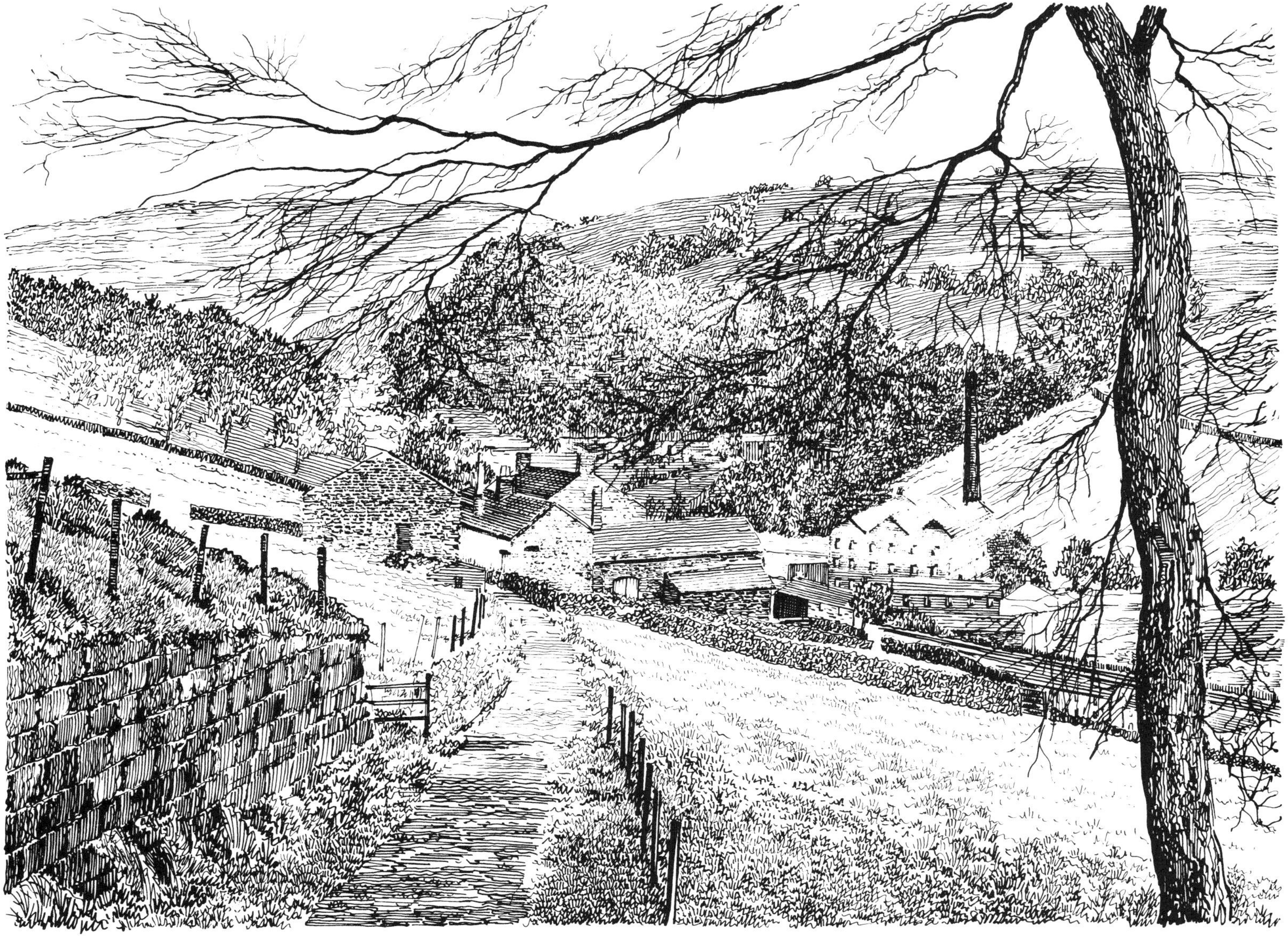

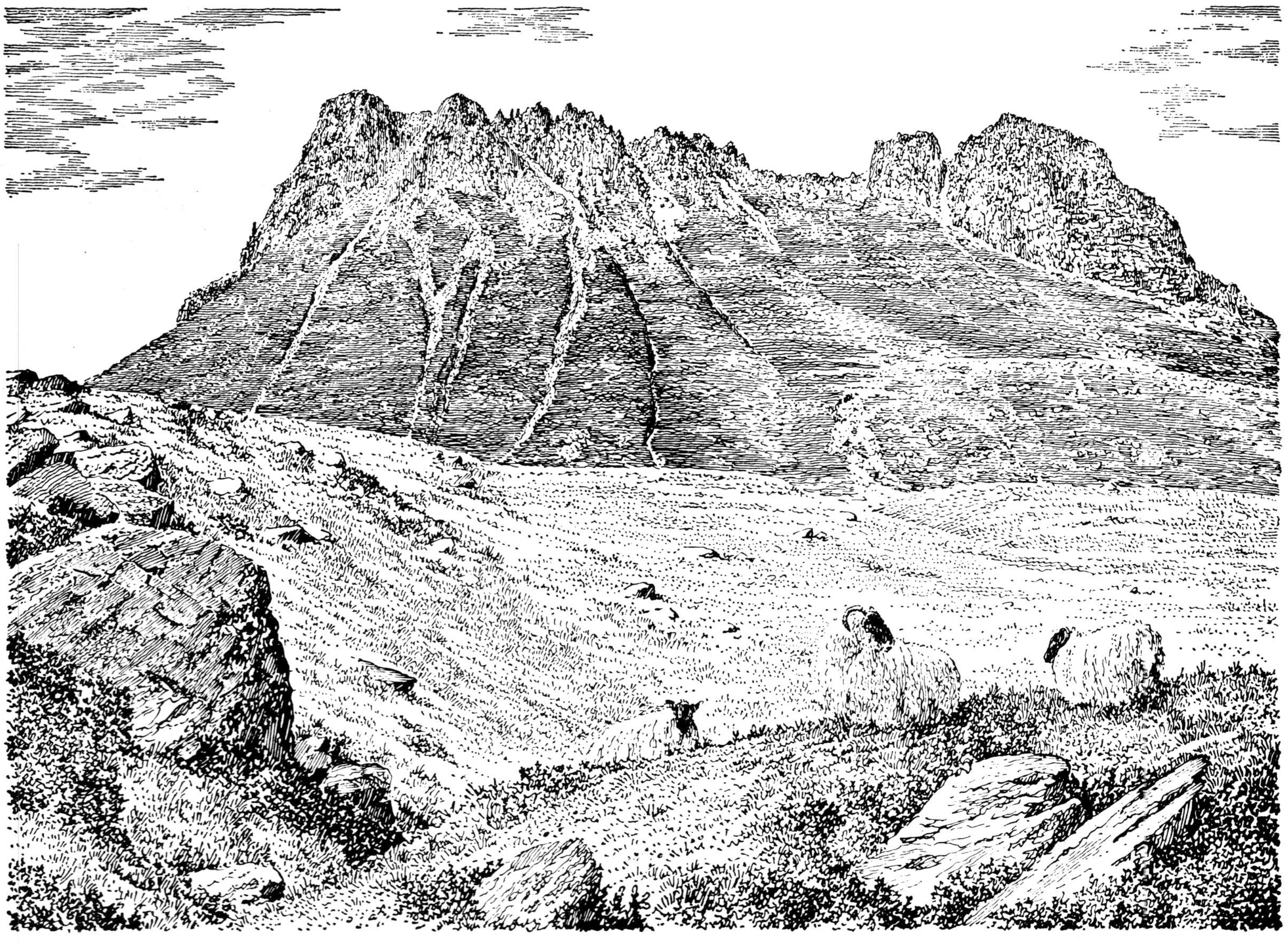

STAC POLLY (STAC POLLAIDH), THE STEEP ROCK OF THE BOG

Visitors to Stac Polly have described its appearance in a variety of imaginative phrases but nobody has bettered Professor Heddle's vivid description of it as 'a porcupine in a state of extreme irascibility'. Its pinnacled and shattered crest is a remarkable example of the effect of weather erosion on sandstone. The word 'unique' is one to use sparingly: here it is very apt. There is no other mountain like Stac Polly.

E

E

E

DERWENTWATER
The viewpoint is Brandelhow and the occasion the wonderful winter of 1963–4, when for months Lakeland was gripped by an unbroken frost under cloudless skies. Derwentwater was a sheet of ice from end to end, the surface being mantled in snow: a truly glorious scene.

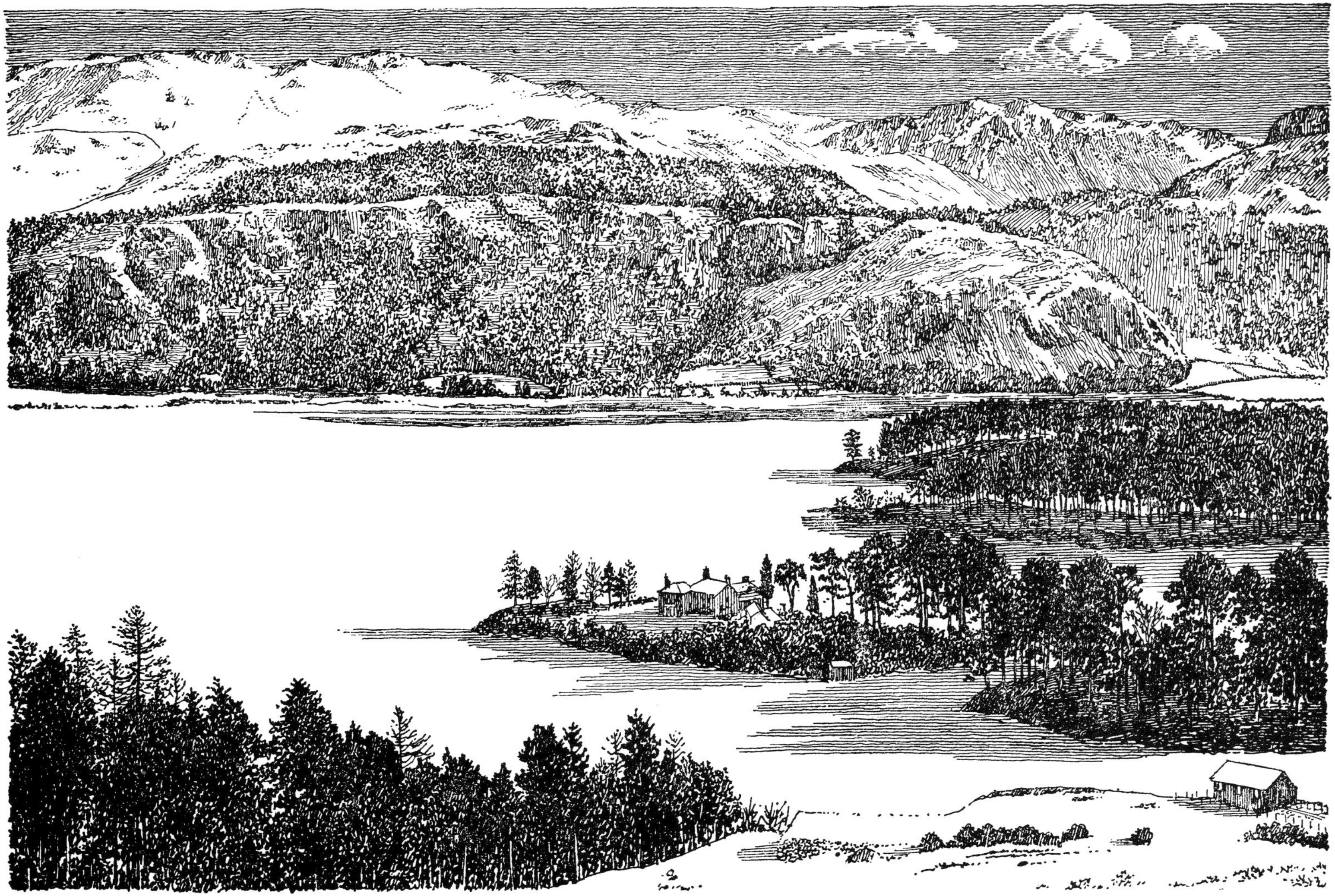

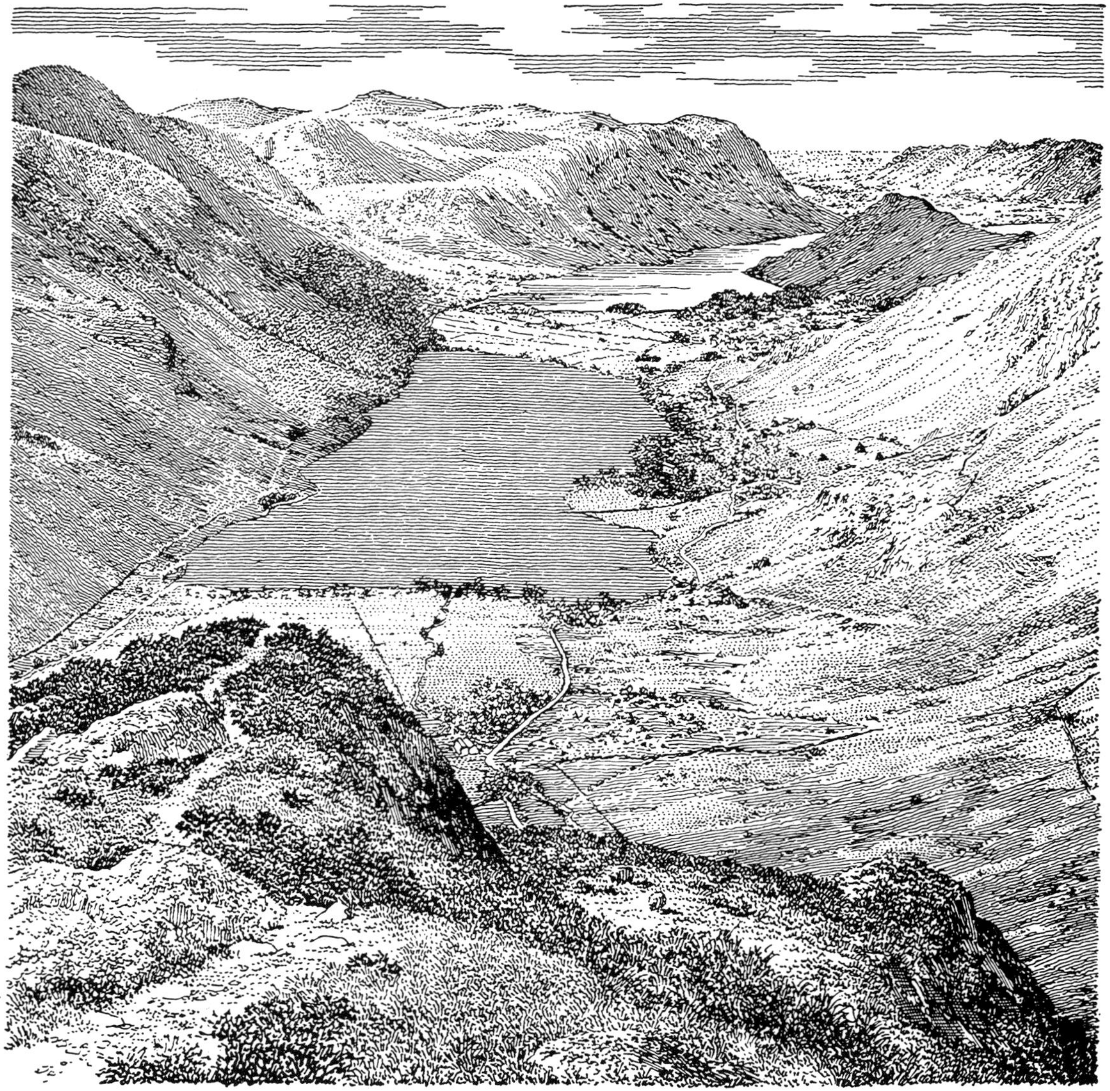

F

THE BUTTERMERE VALLEY

F

F

F

LANGDALE PIKES, FROM LINGMOOR FELL

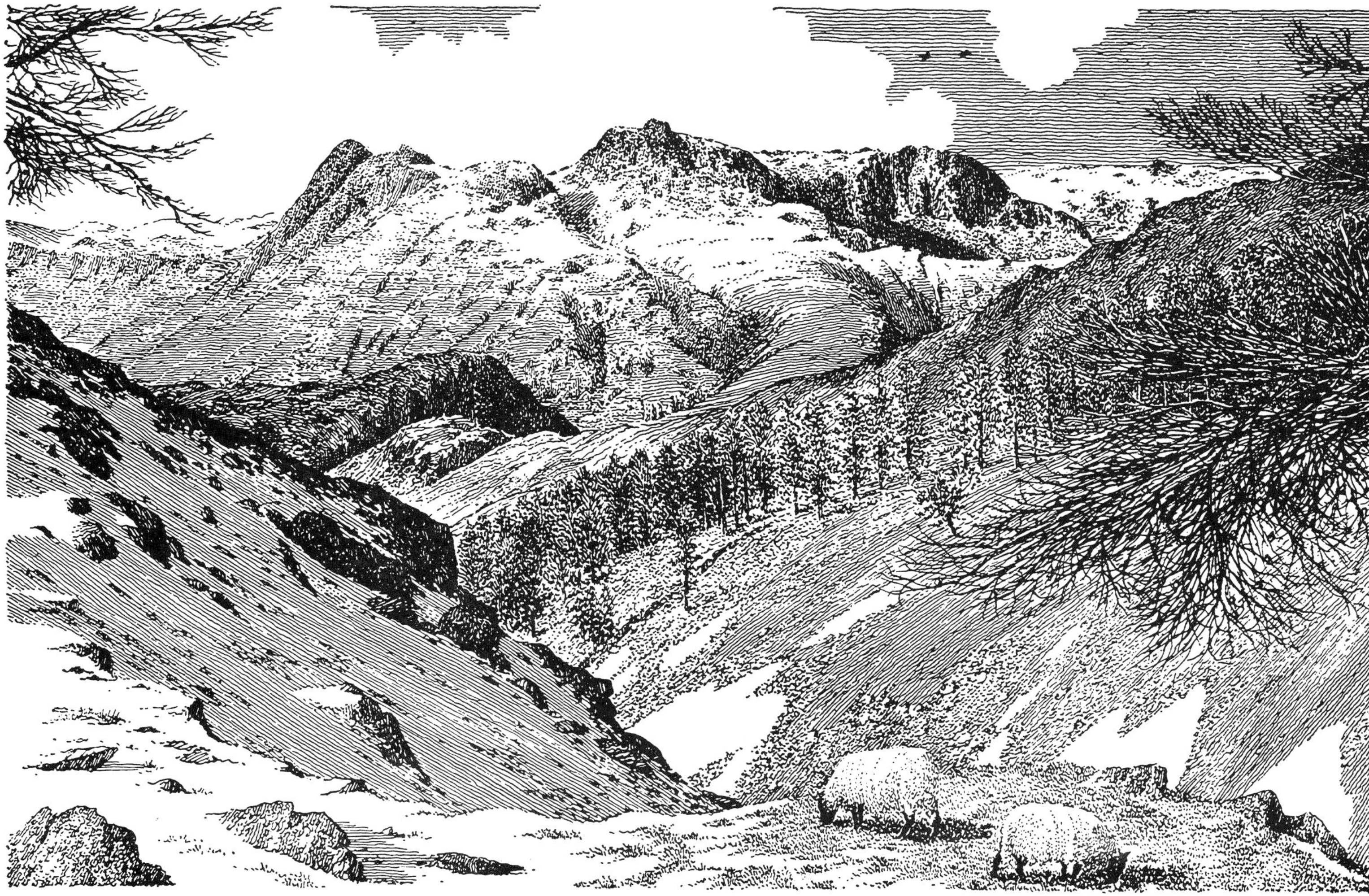

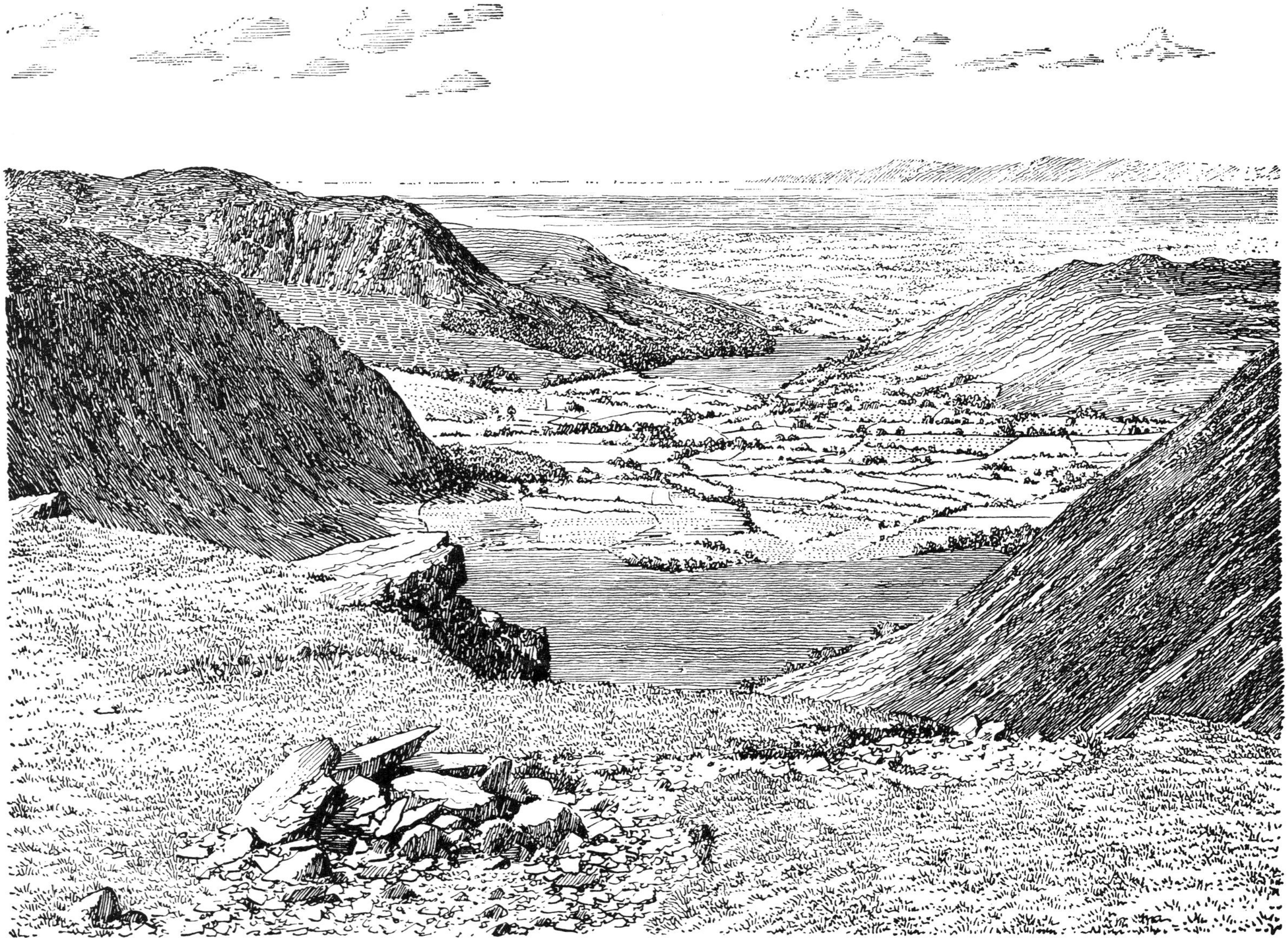

G

THE LOWESWATER VALLEY

G

G

G

THE STRID, RIVER WHARFE
The Wharfe, upstream from Bolton Abbey, passes through scenery of unsurpassed beauty, its clear waters meandering placidly under a canopy of foliage. But at one point the river is suddenly confined to a rocky channel so narrow that an active person can stride or jump from one side to the other, a feat NOT to be attempted. This is the Strid, a notoriously dangerous spot where many lives have been lost. The Strid is a place to see, but not too closely.

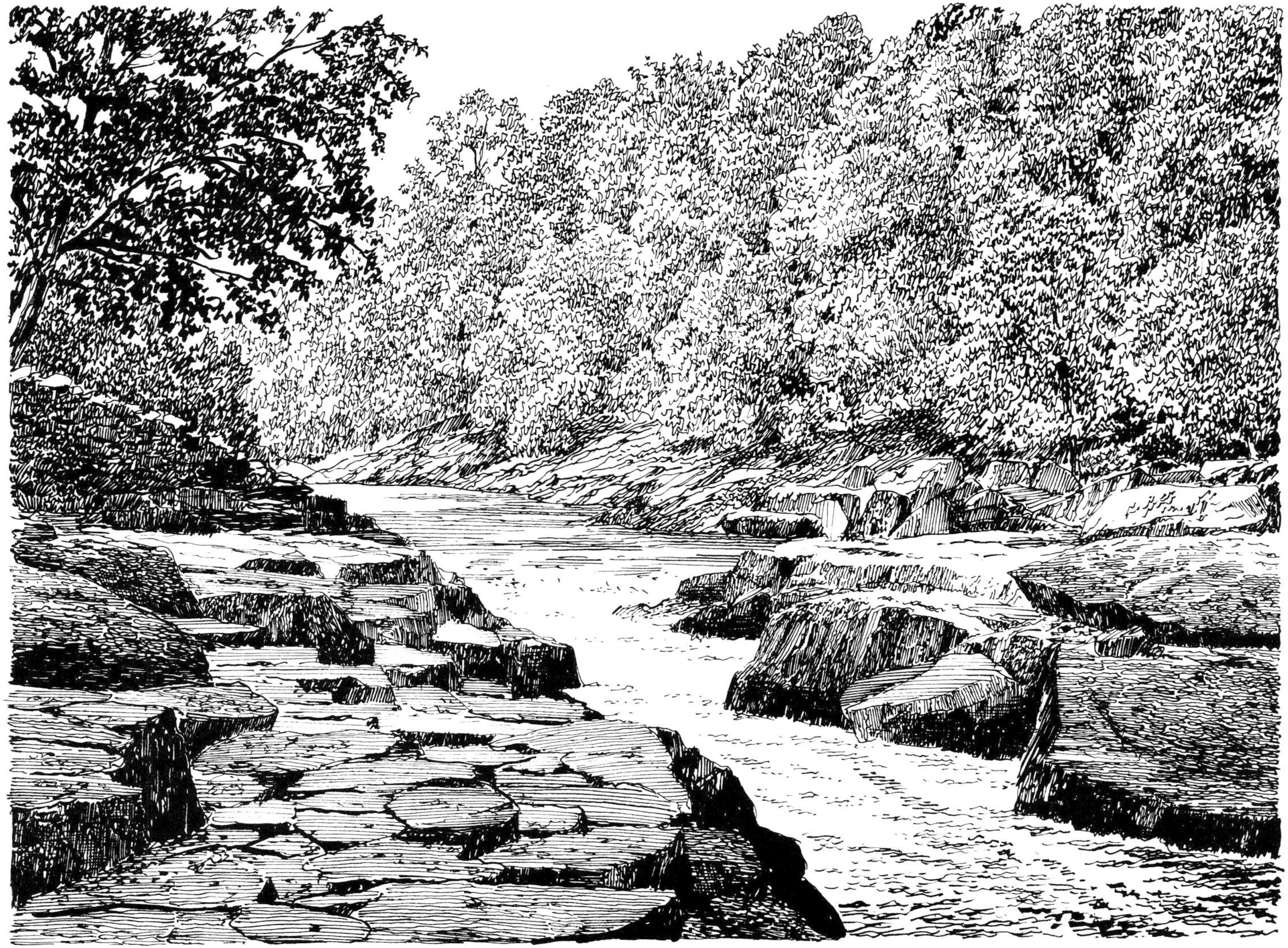

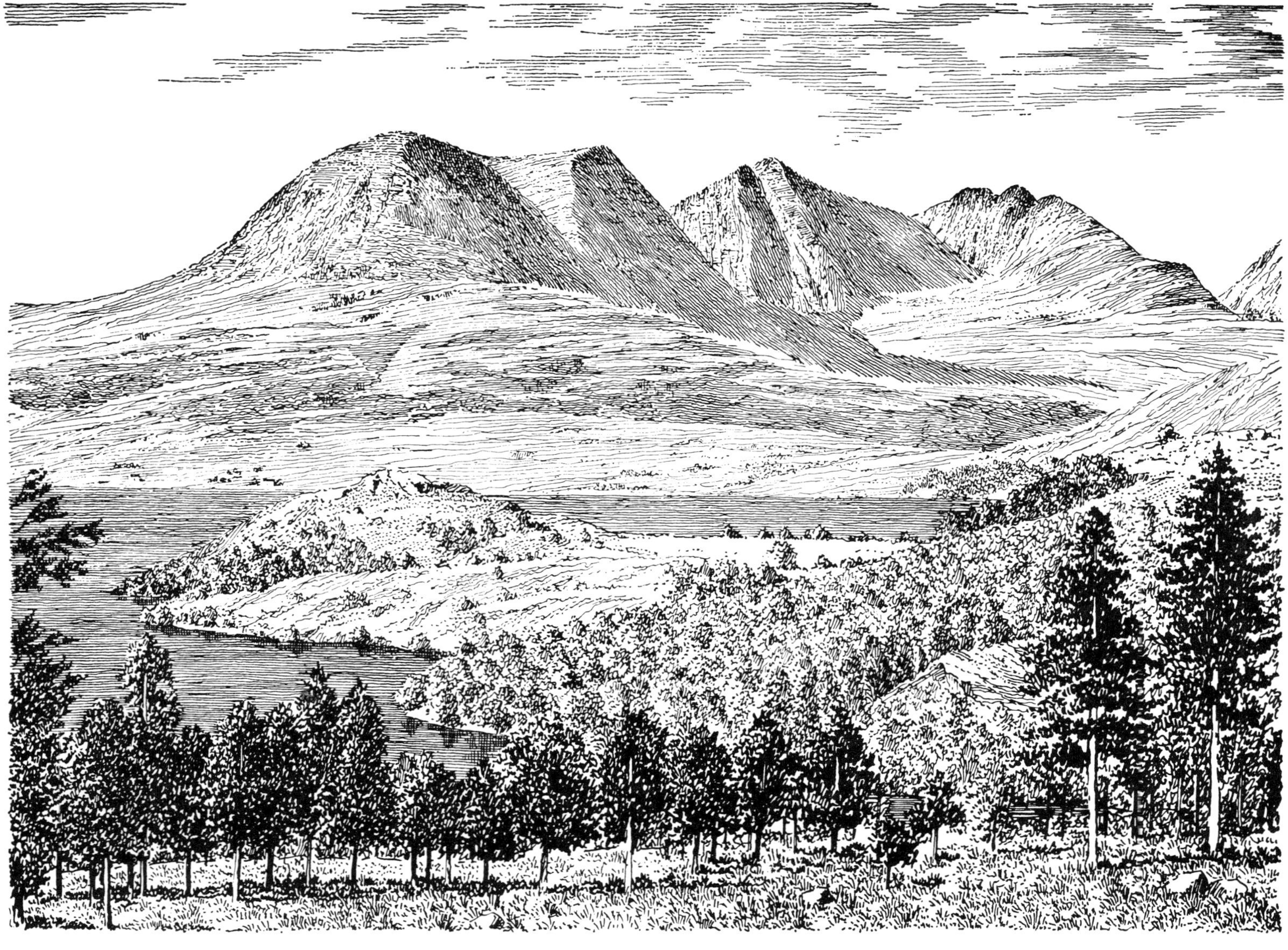

BEINN ALLIGIN, SUMMIT NAMED SGÙRR MHÒR OR SGÙRR NA TUAIGH

The traverse of Beinn Alligin is a popular expedition, and (bypassing its famous Horns) not beyond the powers of the average walker. The summit is a celebrated viewpoint. The mountain is perhaps the most beautiful of the Torridon giants and is perfectly seen from the Shieldaig road, the picture being enhanced by the wooded promontories and lovely inlets of Loch Torridon.

H

H

H

THE PATH TO GREENUP
A path that is a joy on a bright summer morning is the rough track leading up the Stonethwaite valley towards the hills. It is untidy and stony, winding its way amongst boulders and tumbledown walls and bracken with the tree-fringed beck nearby, but as a prelude to a day on the tops it is perfect.

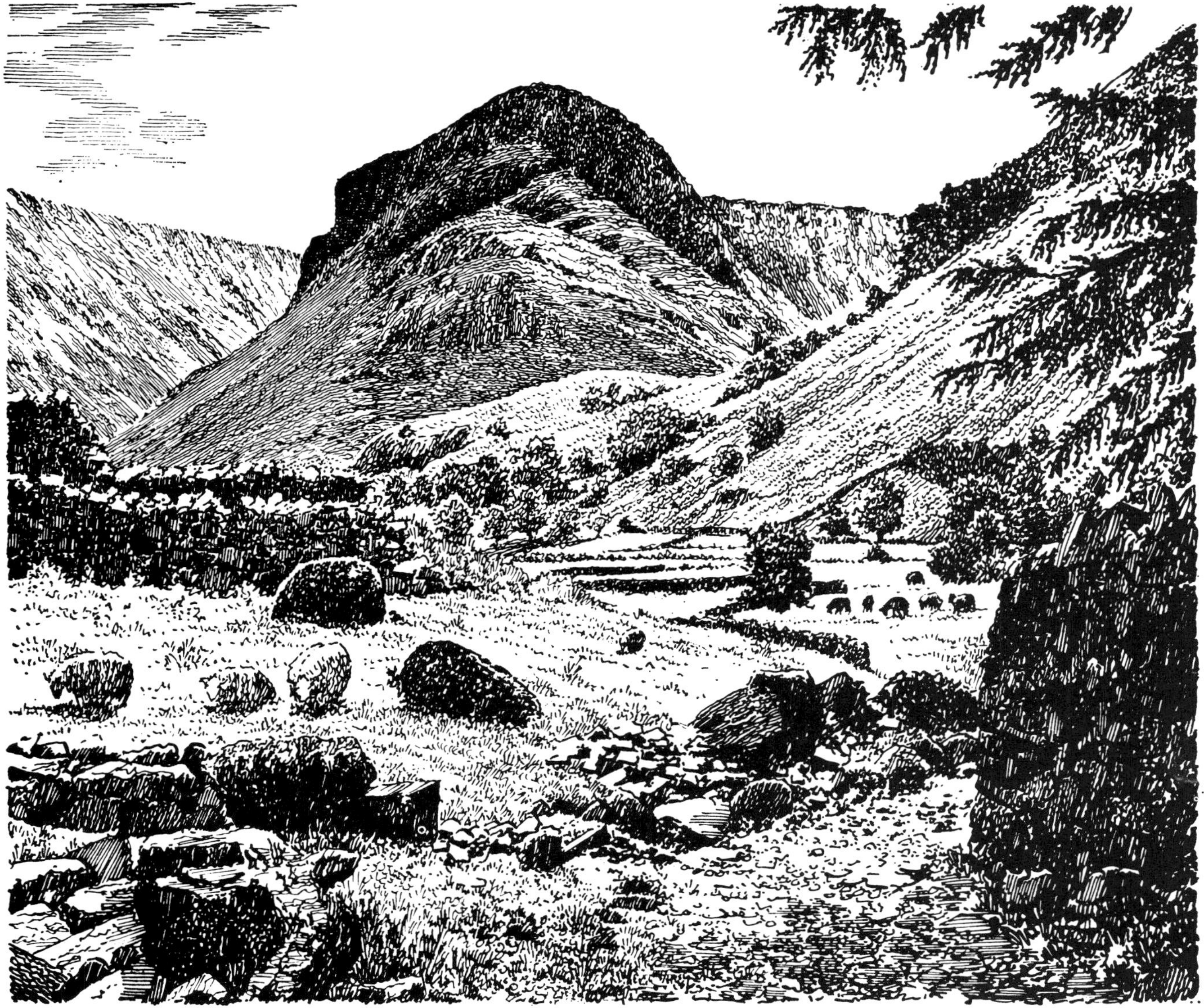

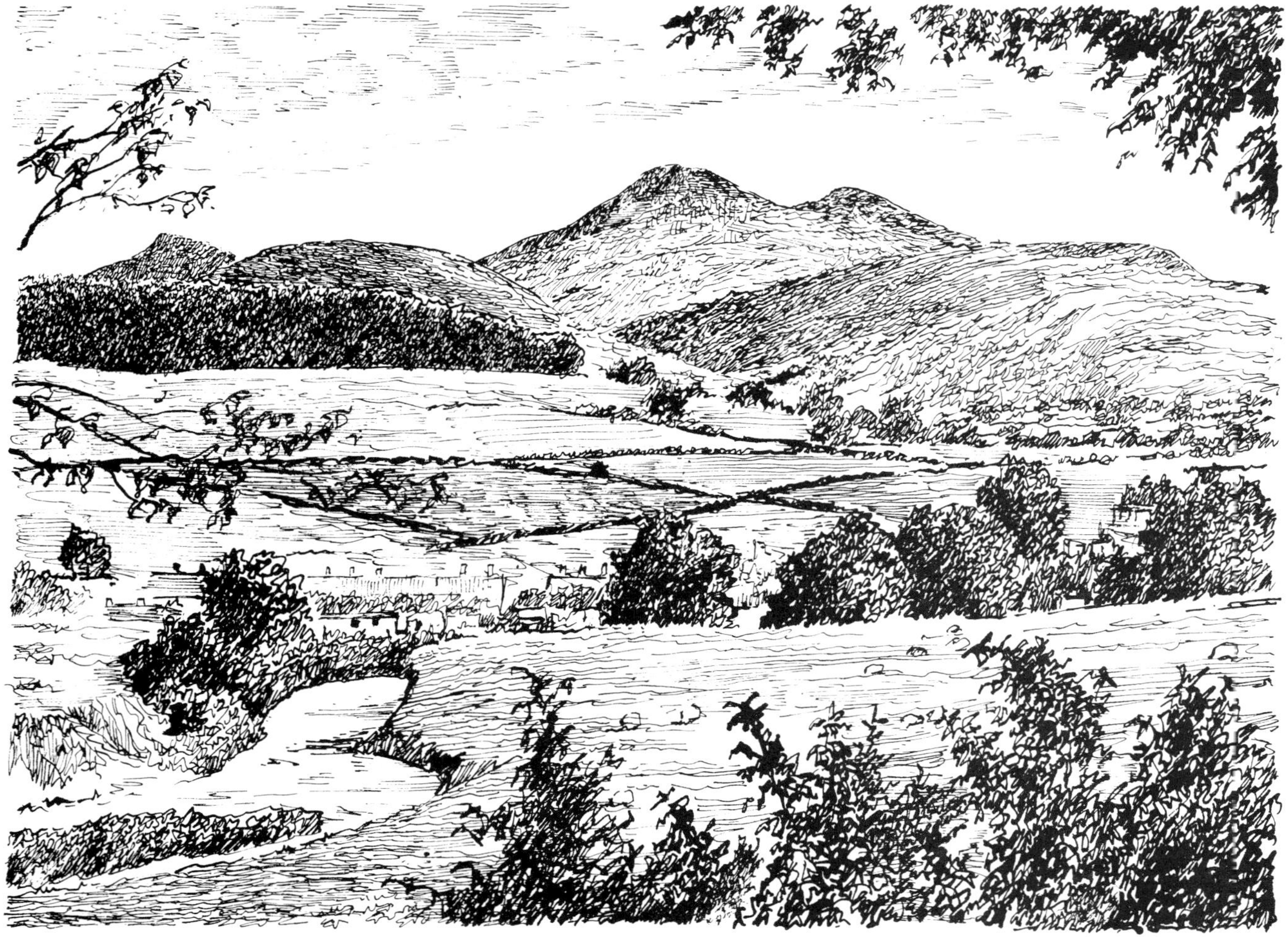

THE BRECON BEACONS
From whatever direction seen, the Brecon Beacons rise in stately grandeur over a wide area of the National Park, forming a beautiful background to the verdant lowlands around. The loftiest point, Pen-y-fan, reaches 2907 feet and is the highest ground in Wales south of Cader Idris. The Beacons are an extensive wilderness, used at times for military training, and no place for inexperienced walkers. The viewpoint of the drawing is the Promenade at Brecon.

I

THE MOSEDALE HORSESHOE

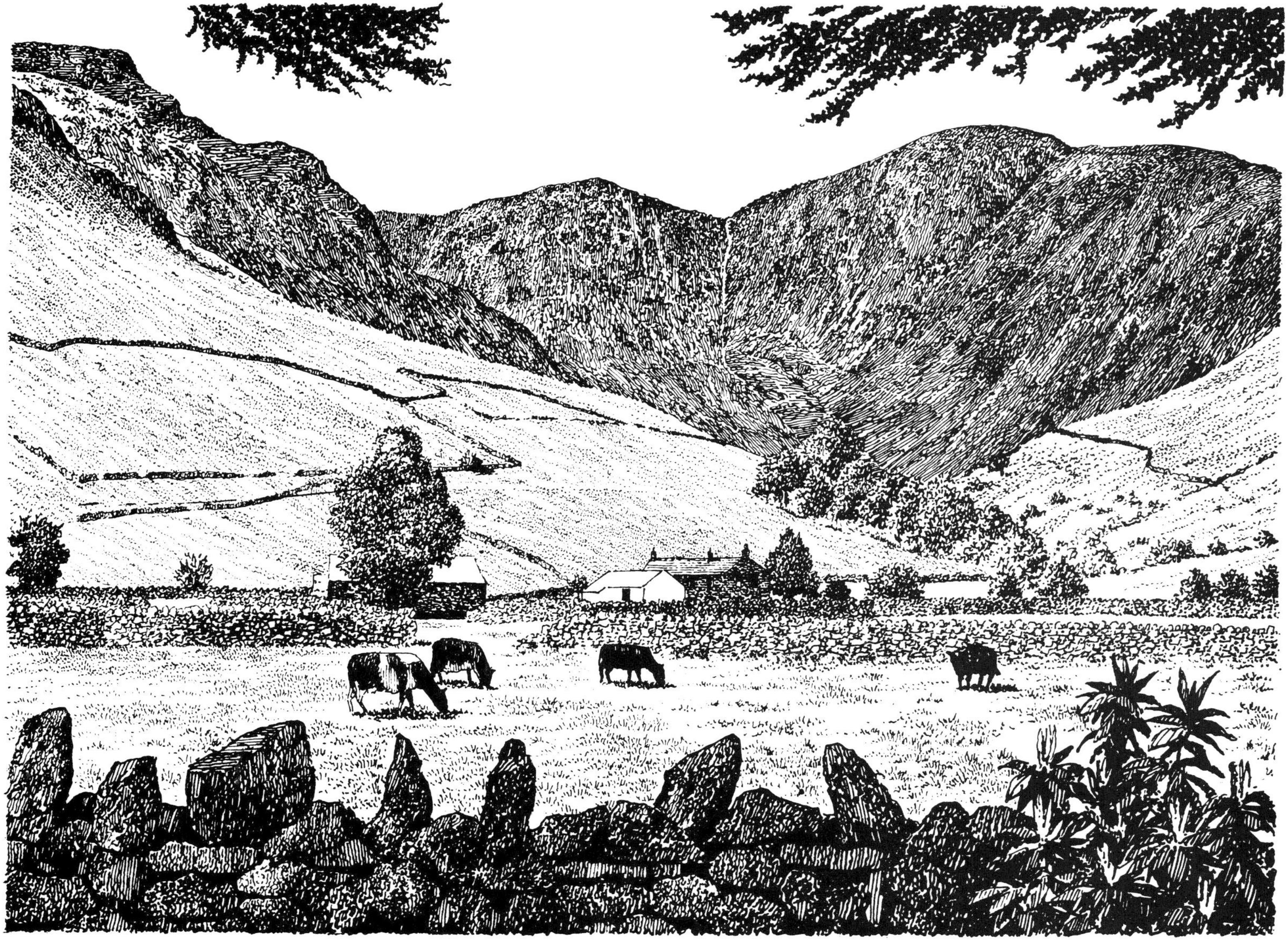

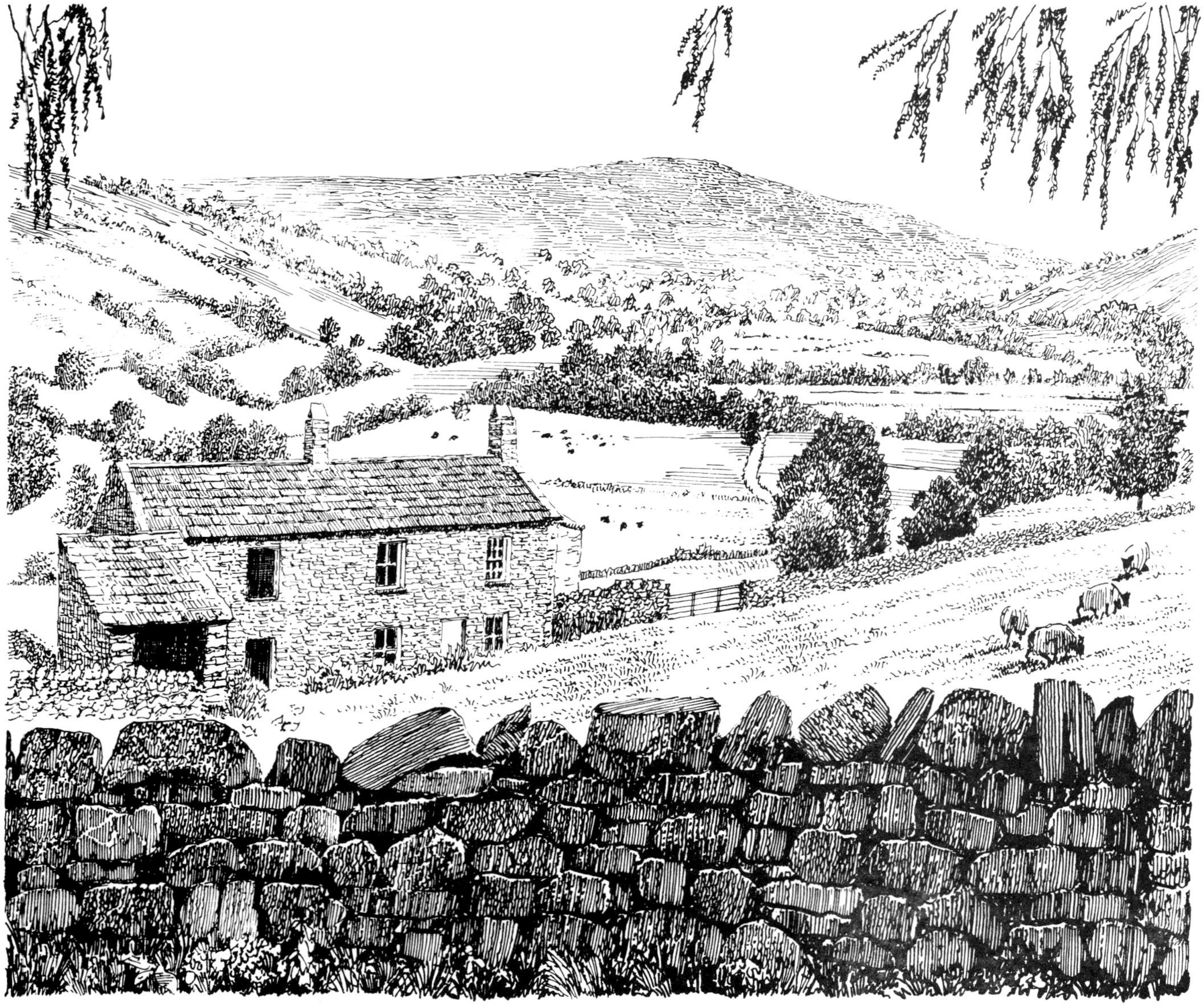

SWALEDALE
If there were to be a poll amongst regular visitors to the Dales to see which valley is adjudged the finest it is probable that weight of opinion would award pride of place to Swaledale. There may be rivers more charming than the Swale, hills grander than the dark moors that border it and sweeter woodlands elsewhere, but no scenes of greater natural harmony, no vistas more lovely, can be found than those that give such delight to travellers along Swaledale.

J

GRASMOOR
The best place for appraising a mountain is a point opposite at mid-height – rarely can its proportions be fully appreciated when viewed from a valley or from a summit of similar elevation. For this reason, the eastern edge of Mellbreak is a grandstand seat for a study of Grasmoor.

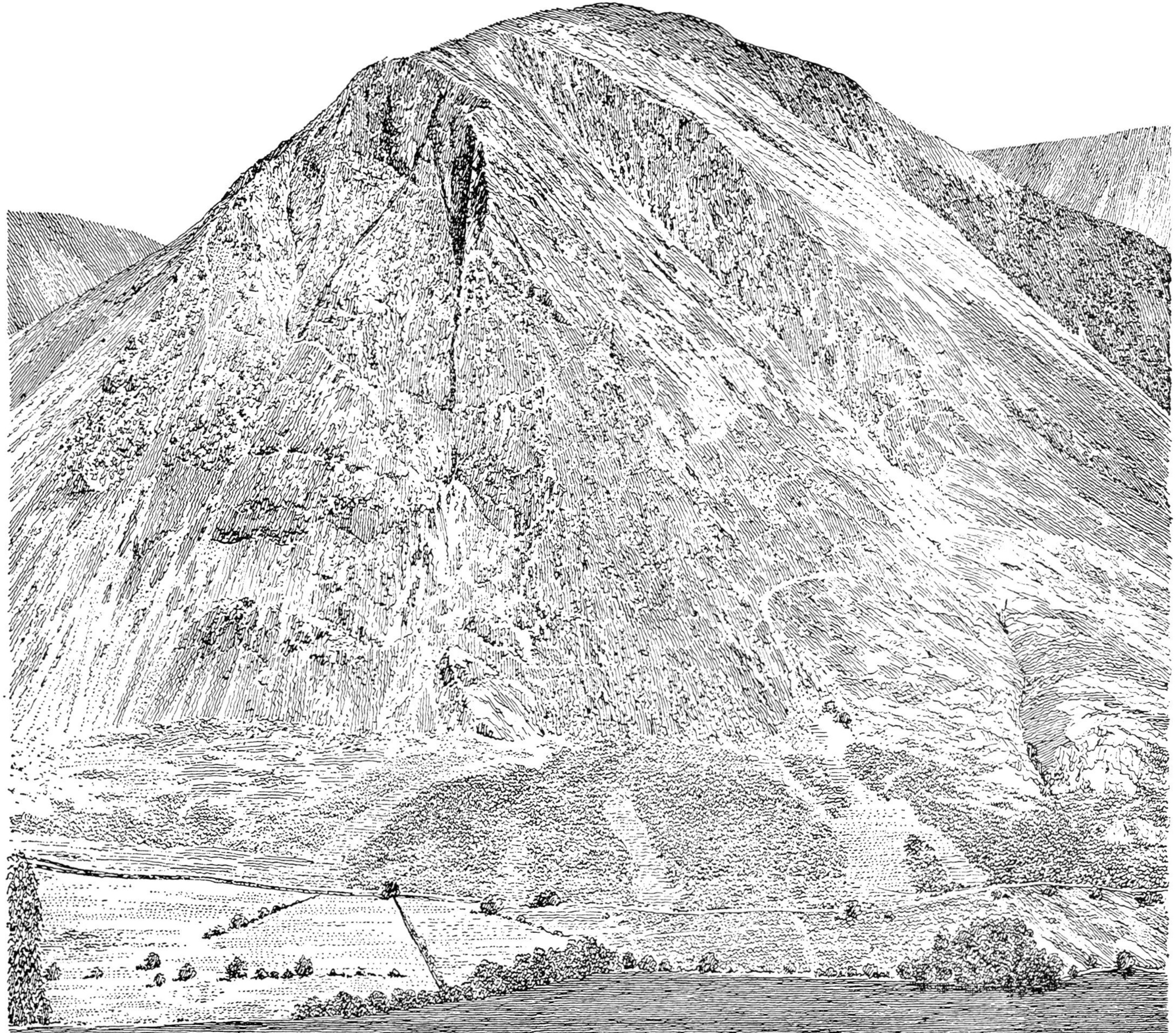

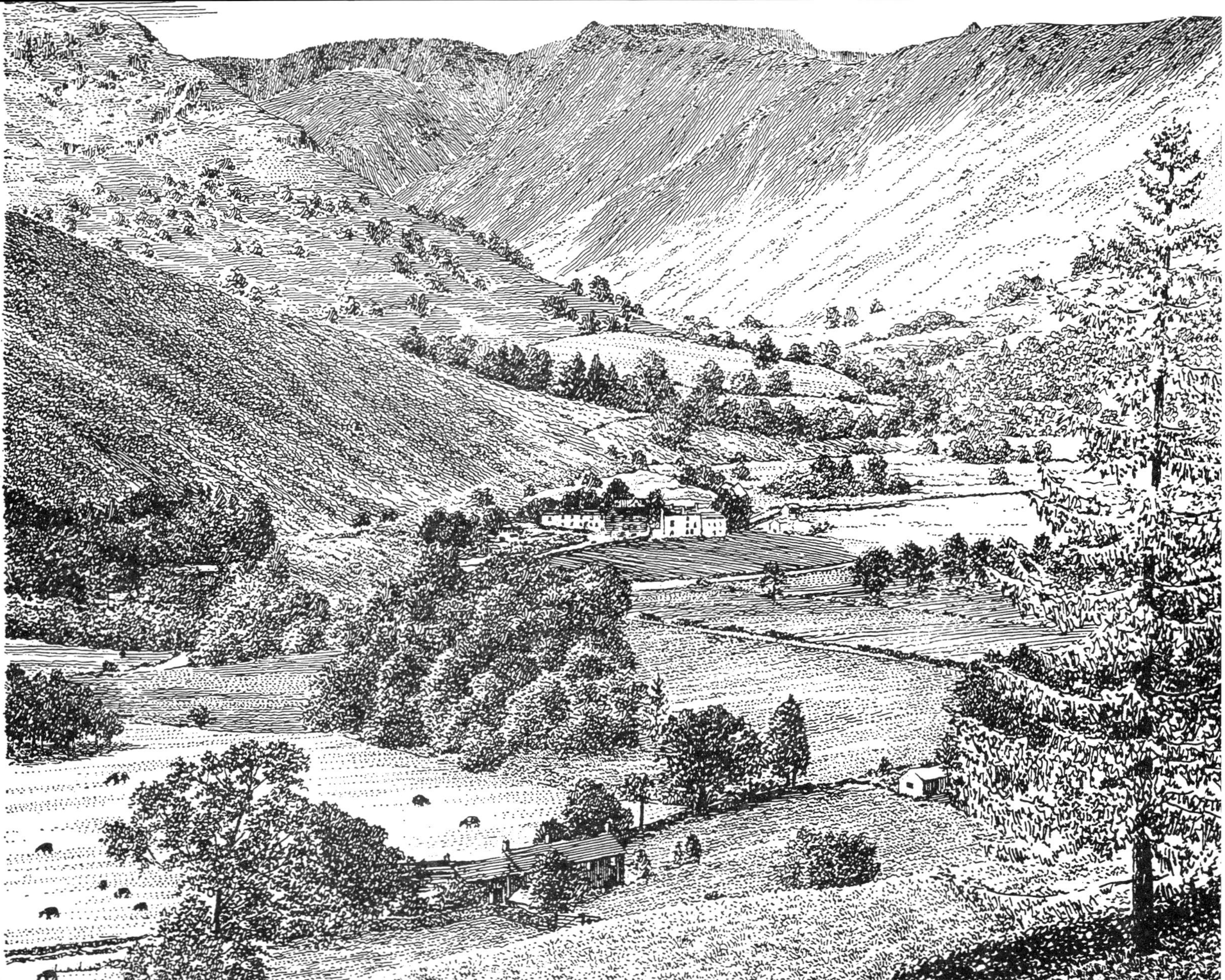

K

THE PATTERDALE VALLEY

K

ST JOHN'S IN THE VALE CHURCH
The tiny church of St John's in the Vale stands amongst trees on the low ridge between Naddle Vale and St John's Vale. Less isolated than of yore, it is no less appealing in its simplicity. At one time it was fashionable for Keswick's visitors to attend Sunday service here, but today's pilgrims carry cameras, not Bibles, to this hallowed place.

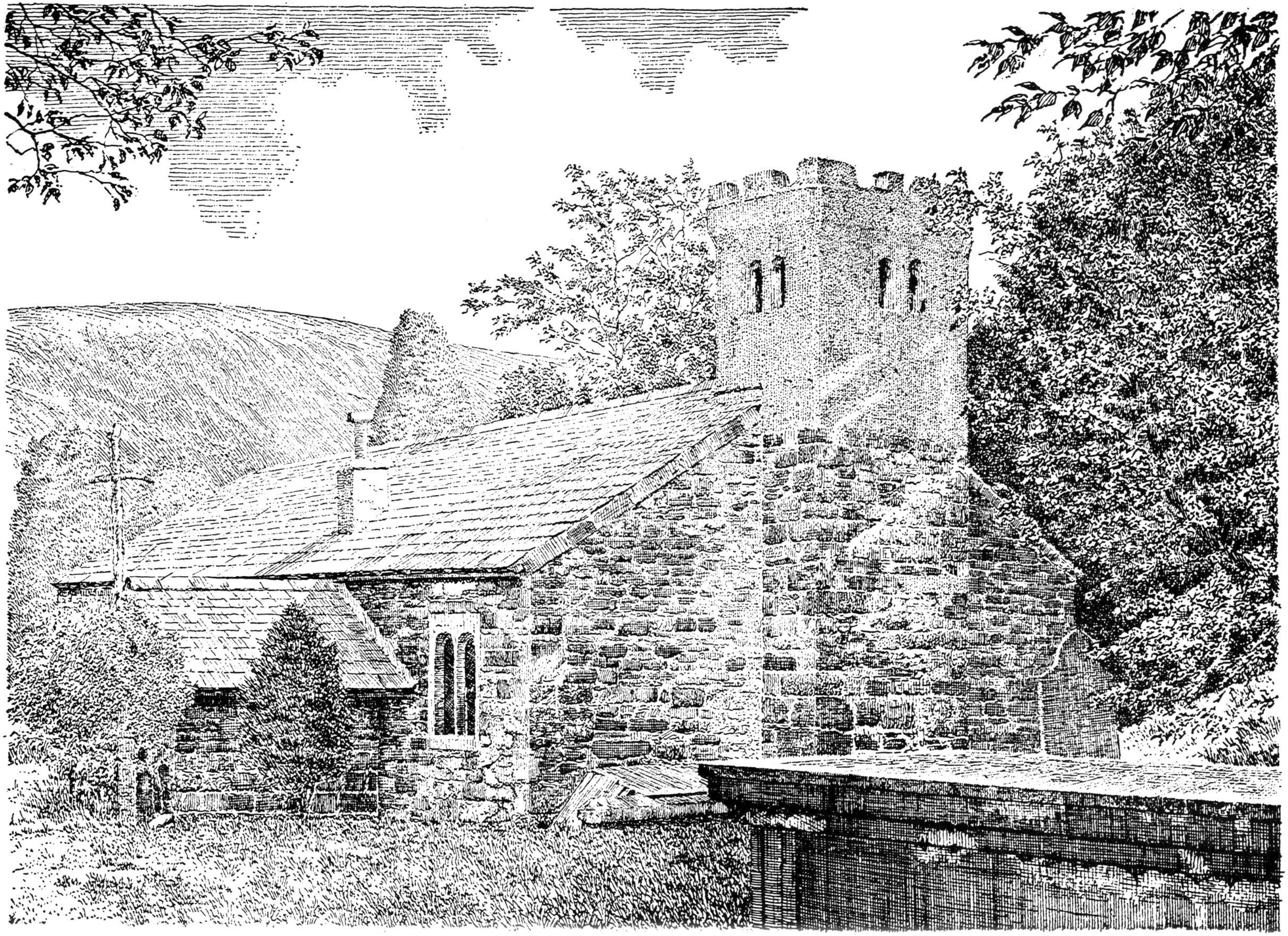

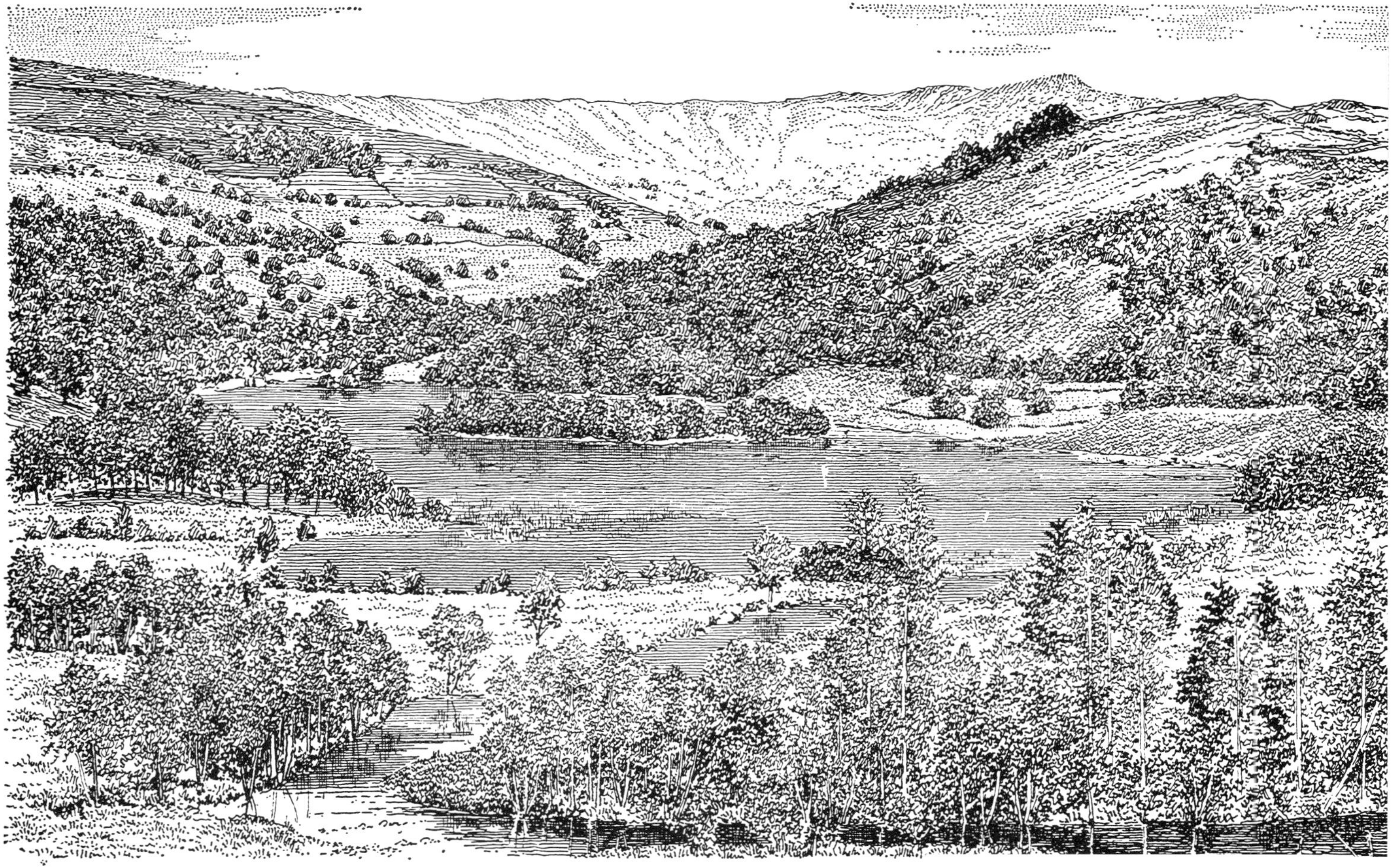

RYDAL WATER
To be factual, Rydal Water occupies the valley of the Rothay between Loughrigg Fell and Nab Scar. But it really needs no introduction. Everybody knows it and everybody goes there. The wardens who collect and remove motorloads of litter from White Moss Common have no doubt about it.

L

L

L

BOWNESS BAY, WINDERMERE
Bowness Bay presents a scene of animation alien to Lakeland, and discerning visitors (in the minority, judging by the Bowness crowds) search for natural beauty elsewhere. Before the tourists came Bowness Bay must have been very lovely. It is still actually rather better than Blackpool.

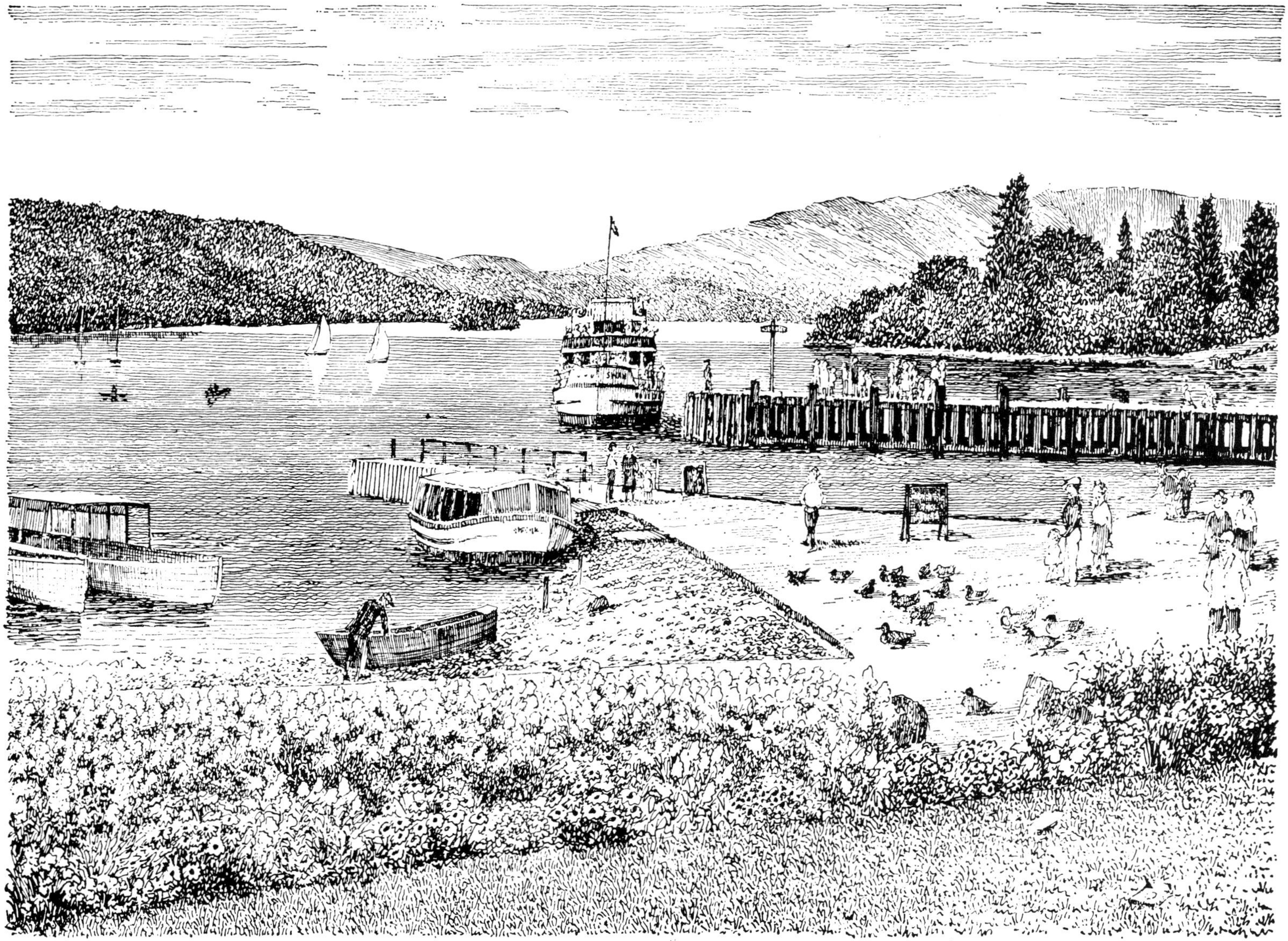

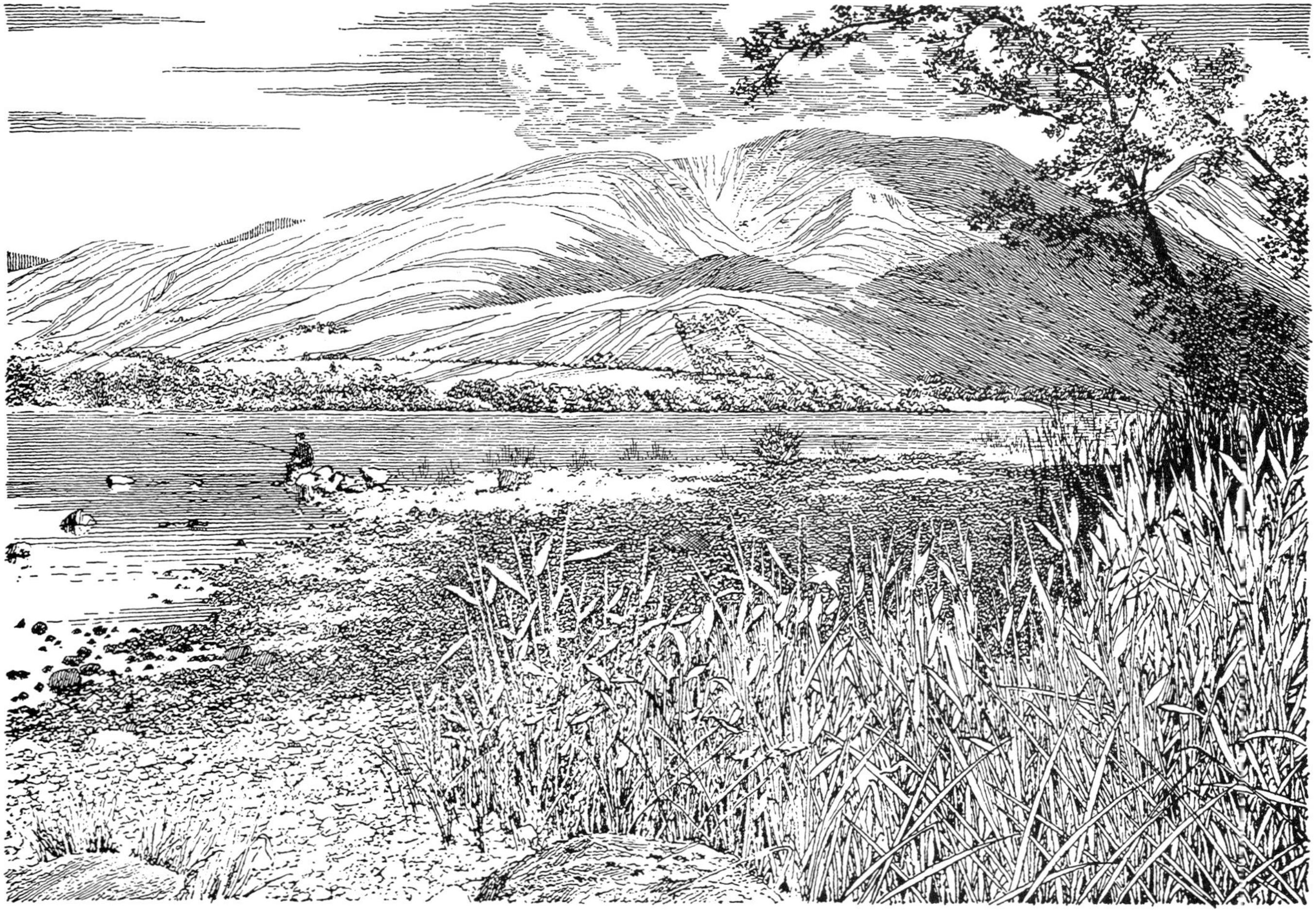

BASSENTHWAITE LAKE
The foot of Bassenthwaite Lake is the haunt of yachtsmen, and their slender craft make a pretty picture as they cruise on its placid waters. The viewpoint of the drawing is the outlet of the lake near Ouse Bridge, where the Derwent resumes its journey from Borrowdale to the Irish Sea.

M

M

M

BLENCATHRA, FROM ST JOHN'S VALE

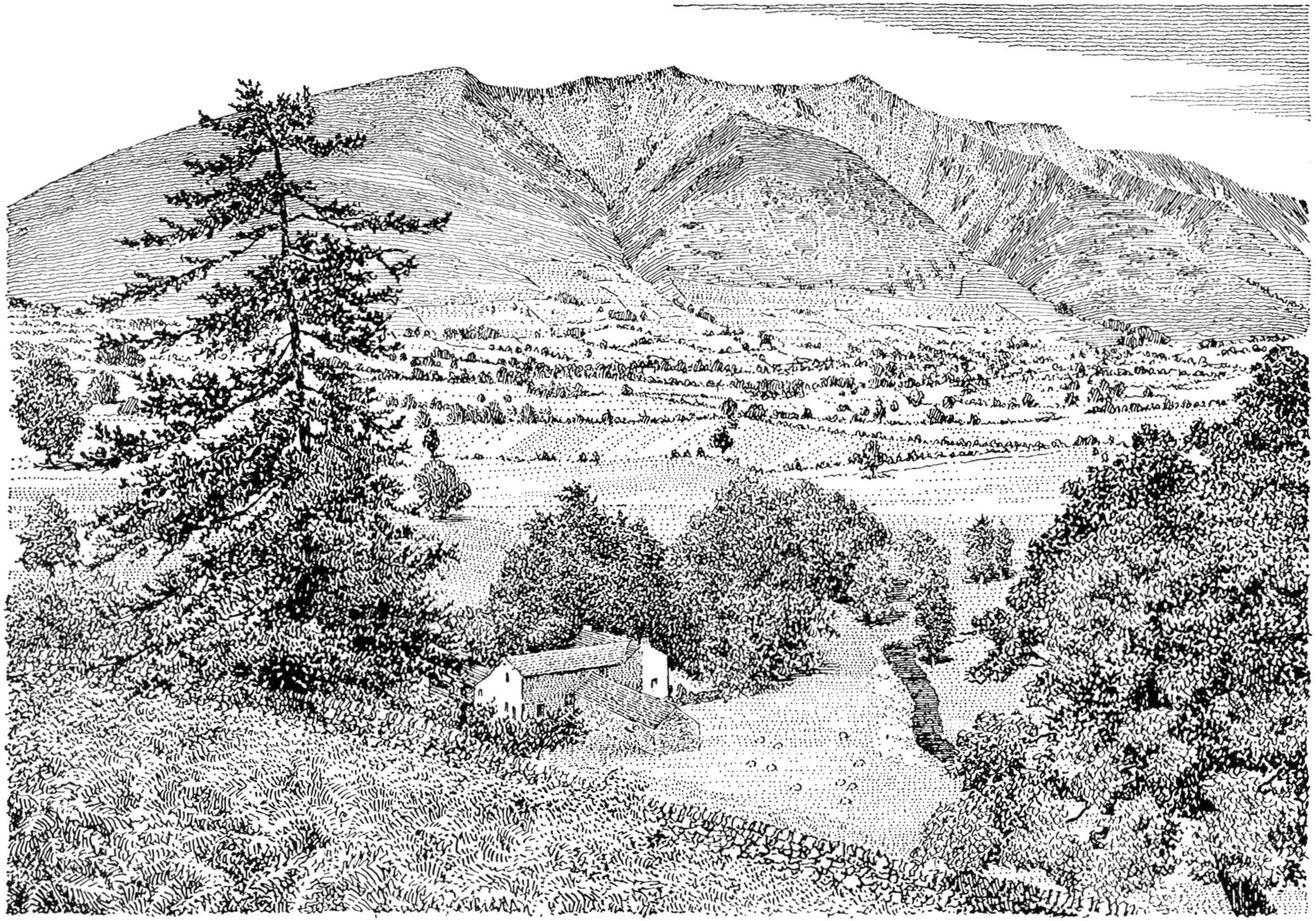

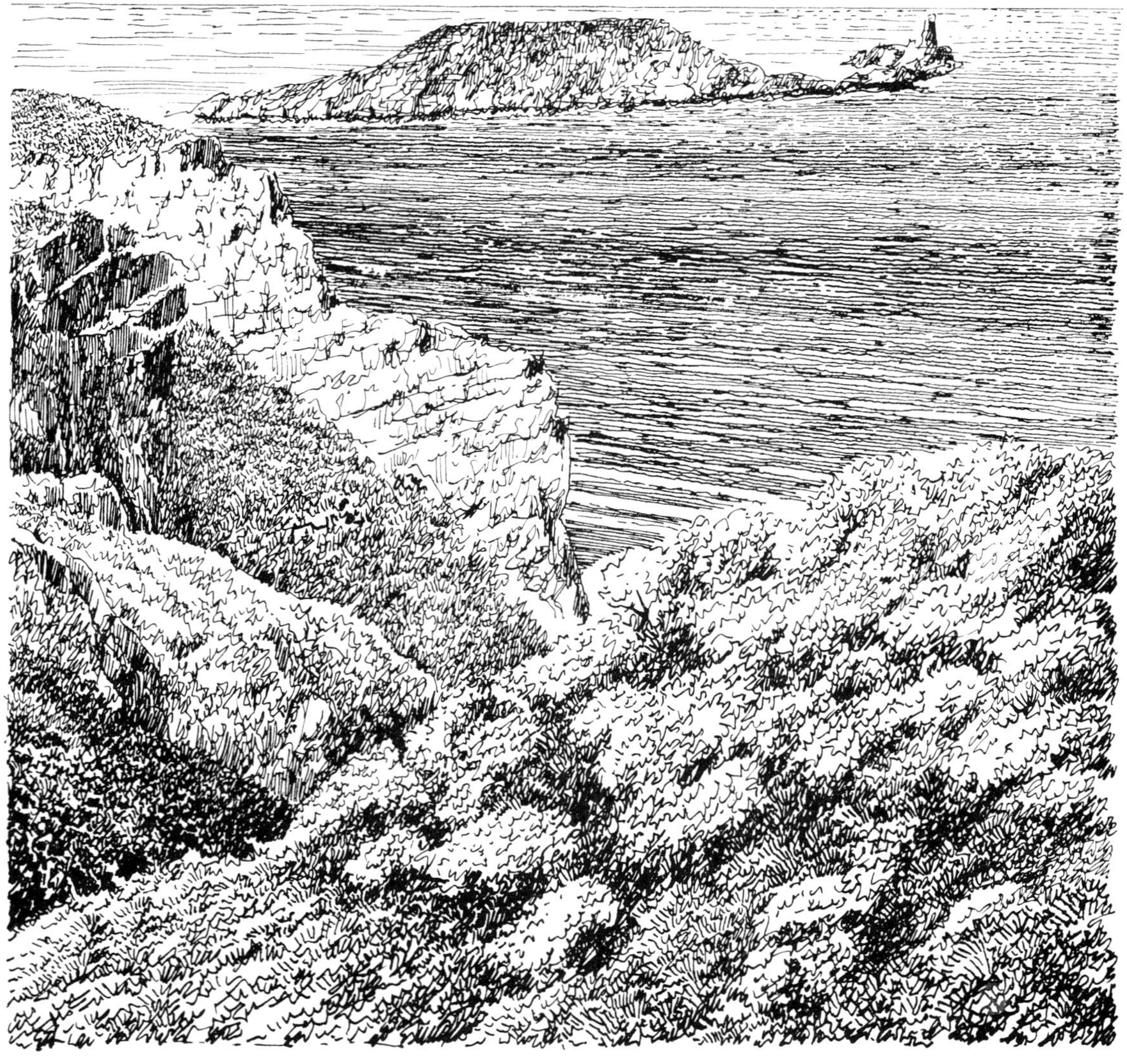

WORMS HEAD
Gower ends abruptly in the towering cliffs of Worms Head and the glorious curve of Rhossill Bay, a fitting climax to a tour of the peninsula. The scenery is dramatically beautiful, and enhanced by a vivid carpet of gorse on the clifftops, along which there is a popular walk from the carpark at the end of the road in the hamlet of Rhossill.

N

ULLSWATER AND GRISEDALE

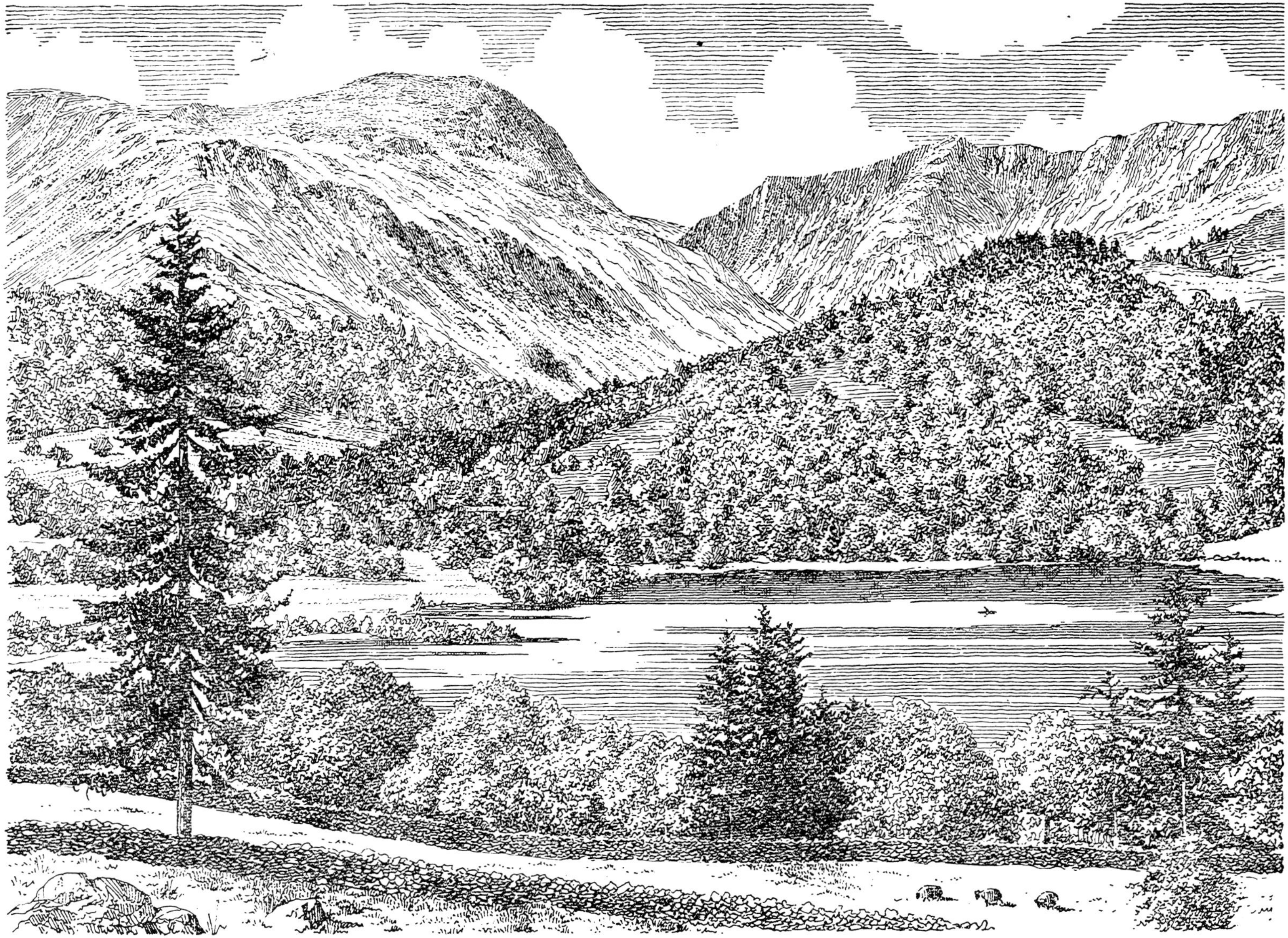

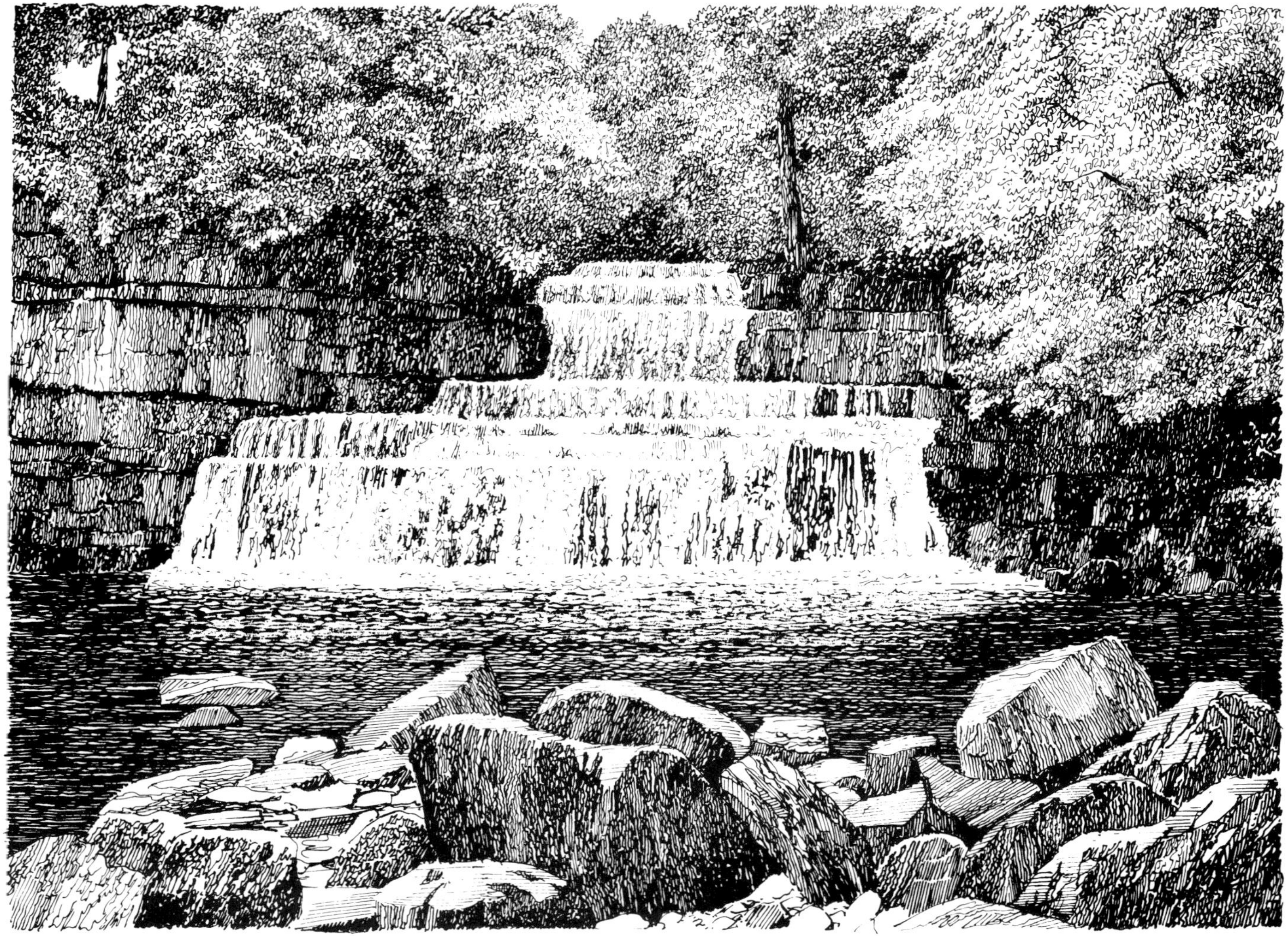

COTTER FORCE
Little known and suffering in patronage from the proximity of the popular Hardrow Force, but well worth the short walk to it from the A684 at the head of Wensleydale, is the lovely stepped waterfall of Cotter Force, displaying its charms perfectly for camera enthusiasts.

O

ROBINSON

Robinson deserves some sympathy for its prosaic name amongst an array of poetic gems like Blencathra and Glaramara and romantic descriptive titles such as Hindscarth and High Stile. It derives from a Richard Robinson, an early landowner, and was first recorded as 'Robinson's Fell'. But what's in a name? This is a grand hill to climb.

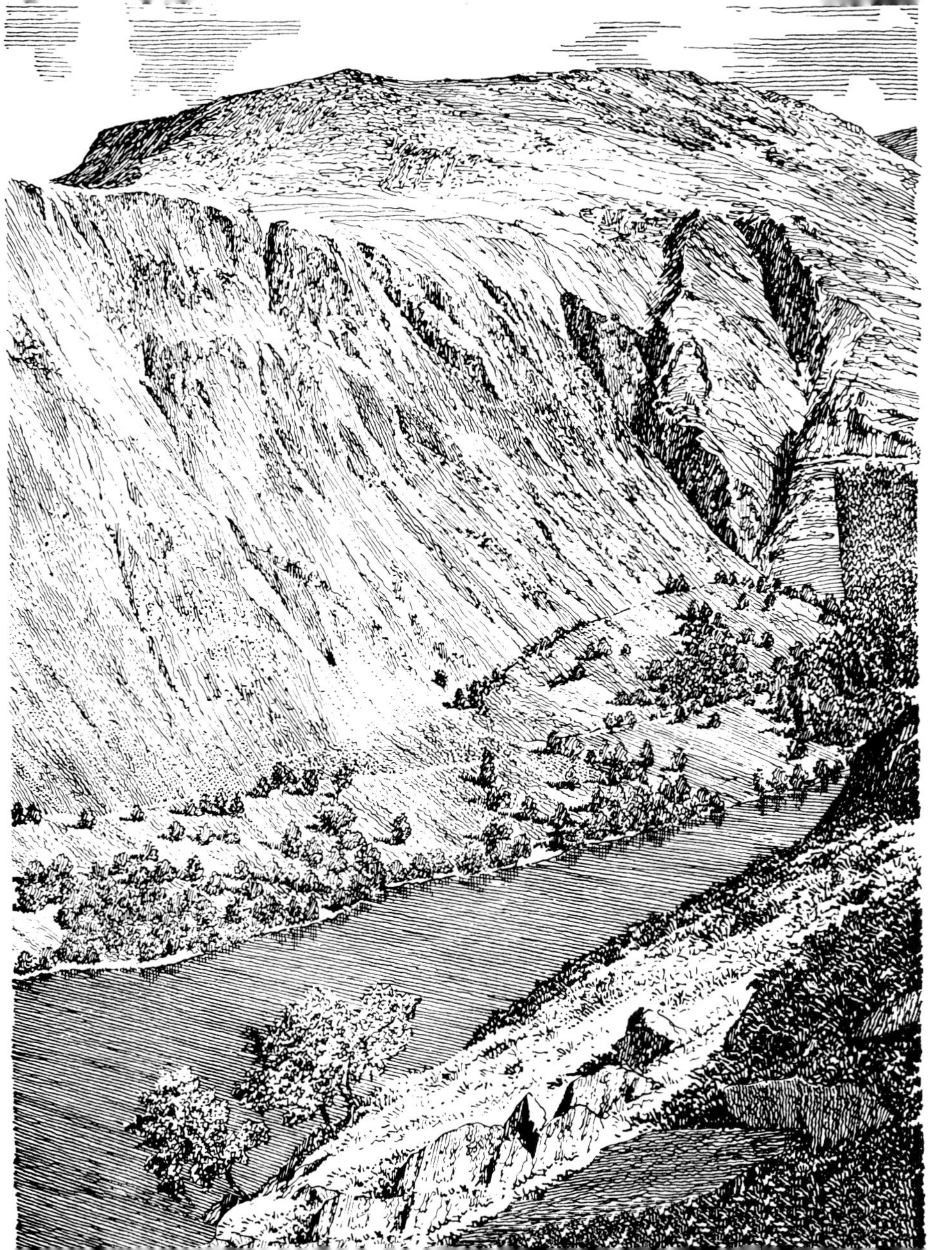

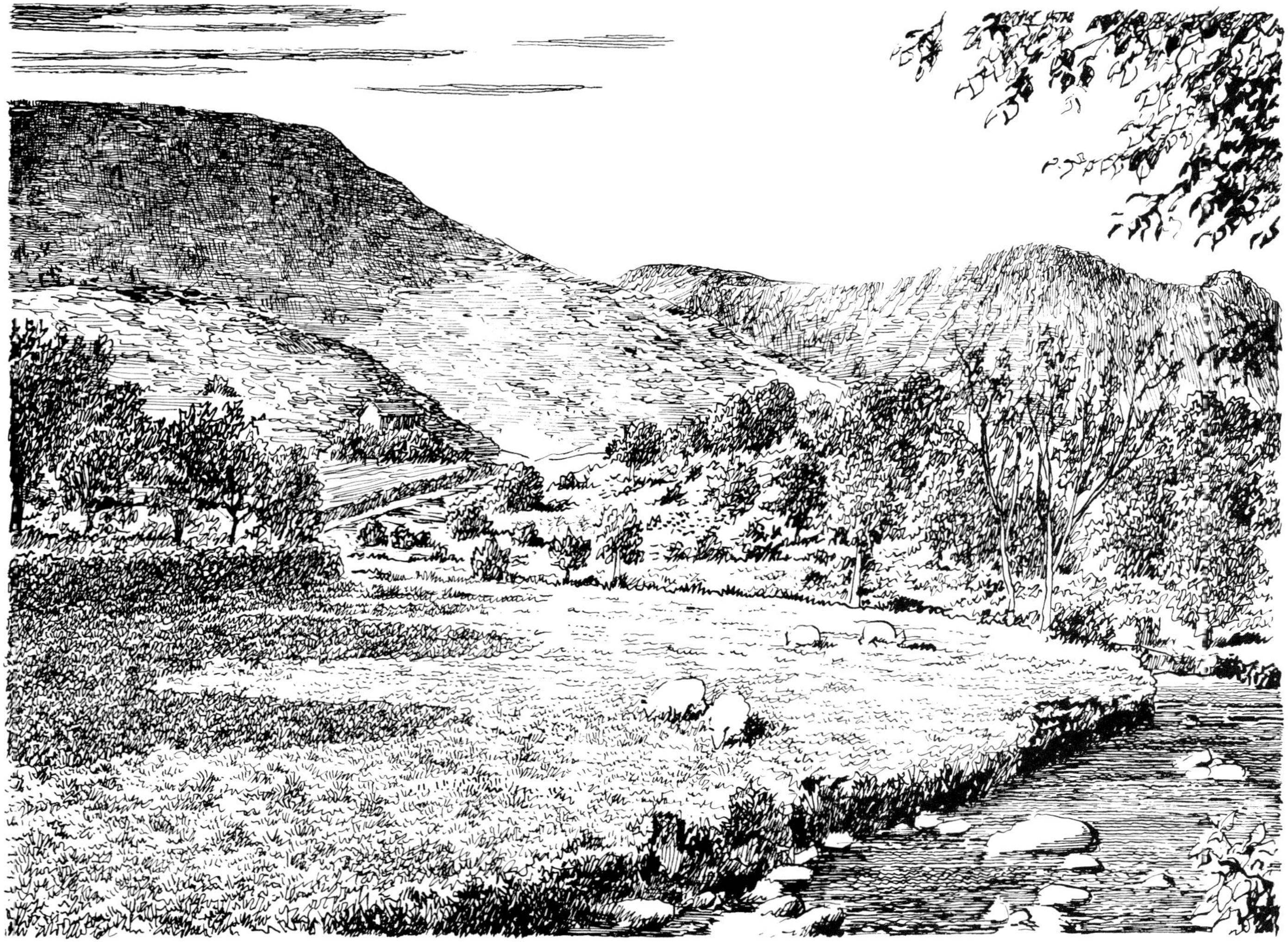

CWM PENNANT

Cwm Pennant, reached from the Caernarfon–Porthmadog road, is one of the loveliest of the valleys of Snowdonia, but, because there is no way for cars through the mountains at its head, one of the least frequented. Better than any detailed description, its charms are perfectly expressed in the words of the poet Eifion Wyn: 'Oh God, why didst thou make Cwm Pennant so beautiful and the life of an old shepherd so short?'

P Q

CRUMMOCK WATER

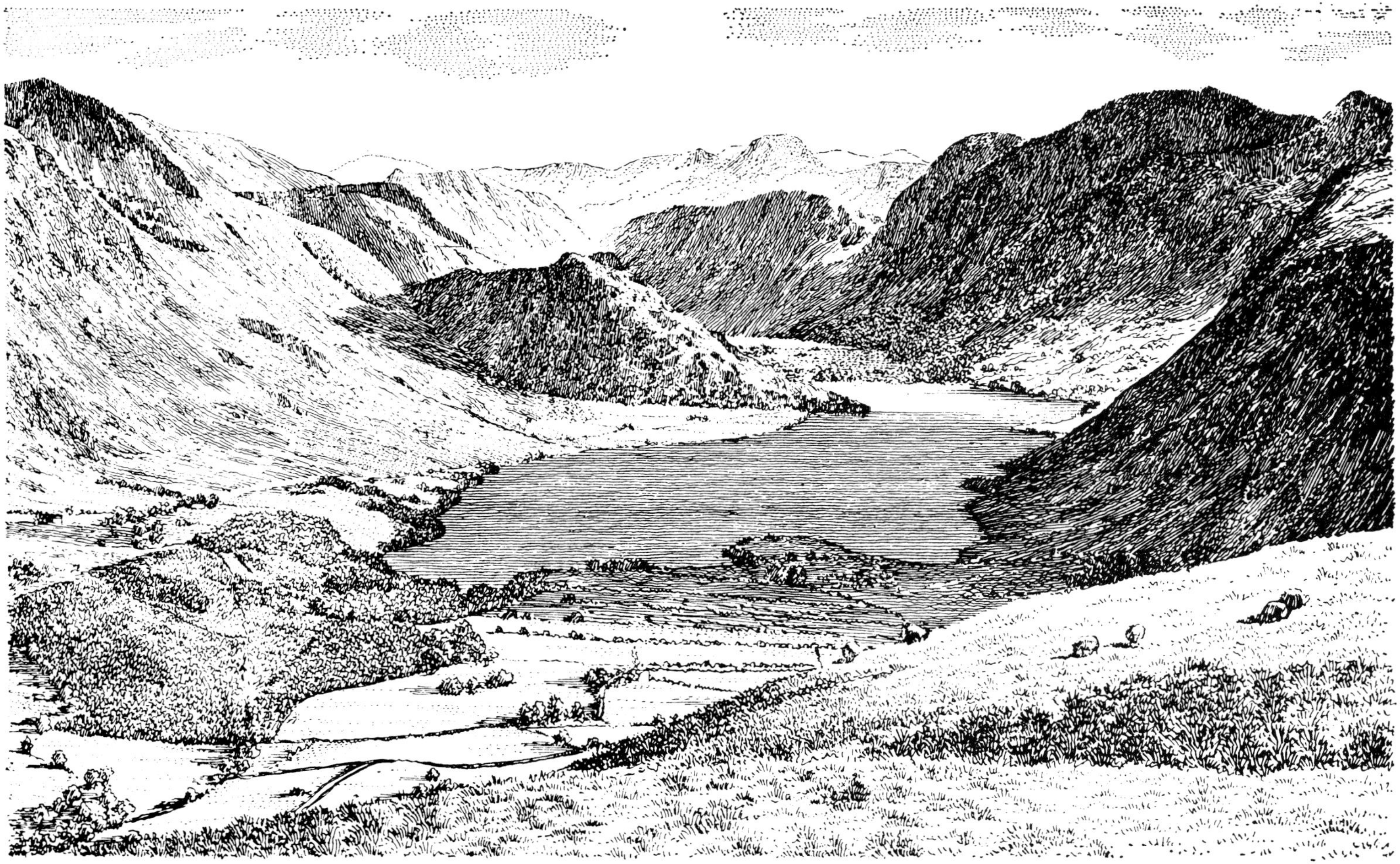

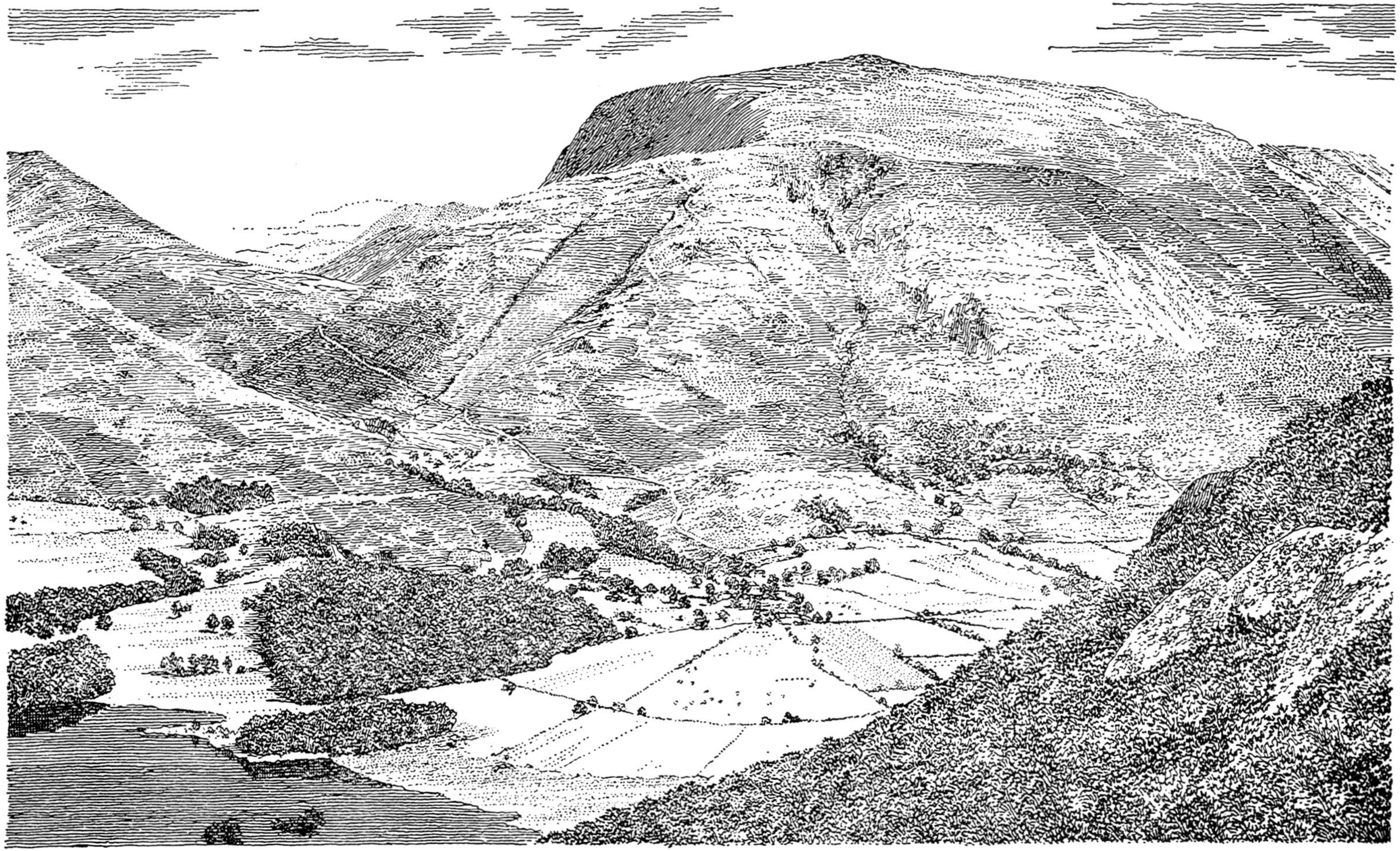

NEWLANDS PASS AND ROBINSON

R

BEN LOYAL (BEN LAOGHAL)
Often referred to as the Queen of Scottish Mountains, Ben Loyal forms a compelling skyline at the head of the Kyle of Tongue, its succession of granite peaks towering almost grotesquely above the surrounding moorlands in magnetically attractive array. From the old road by Lochan Hacoin it presents a perfect picture, much photographed.

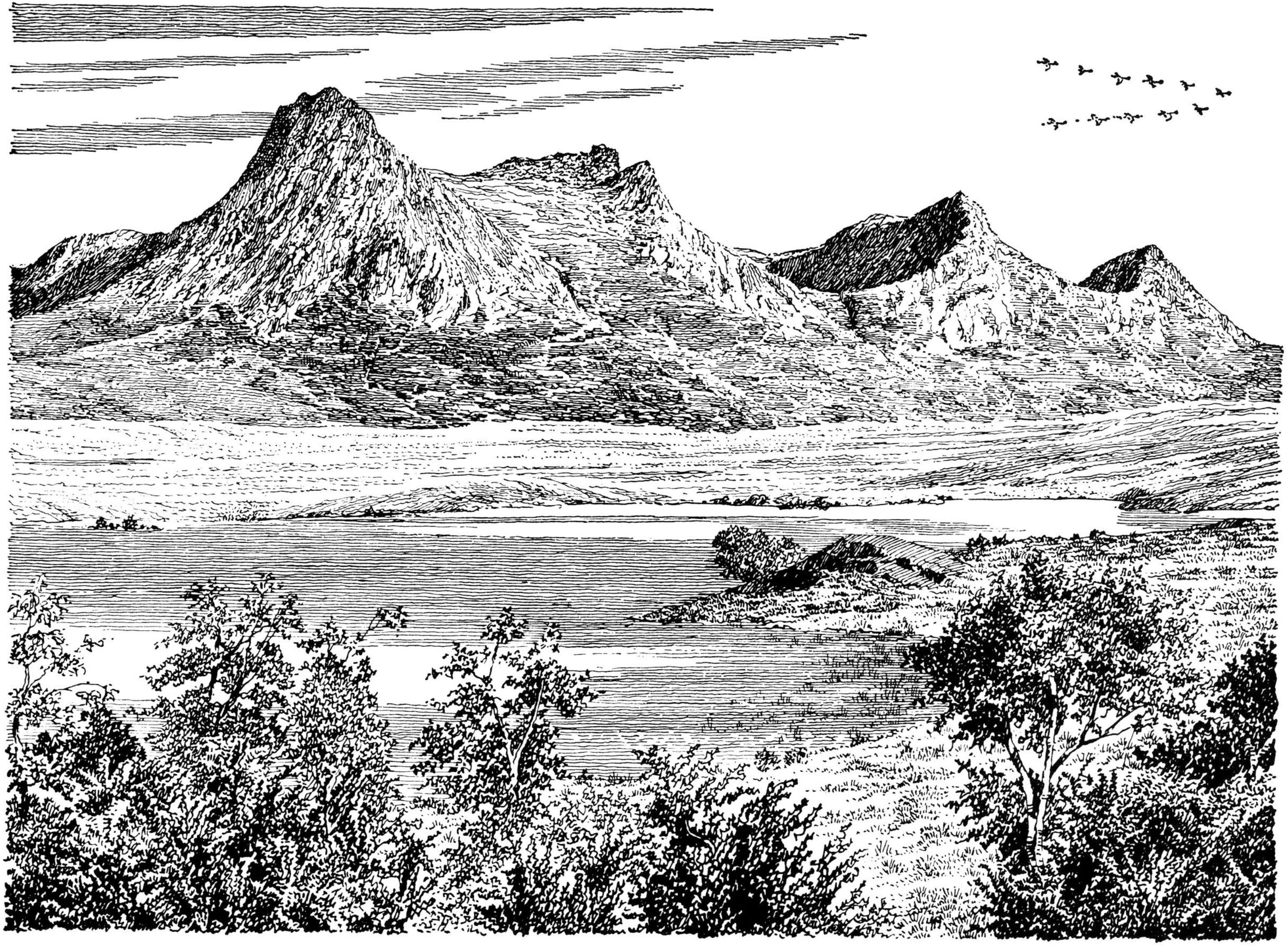

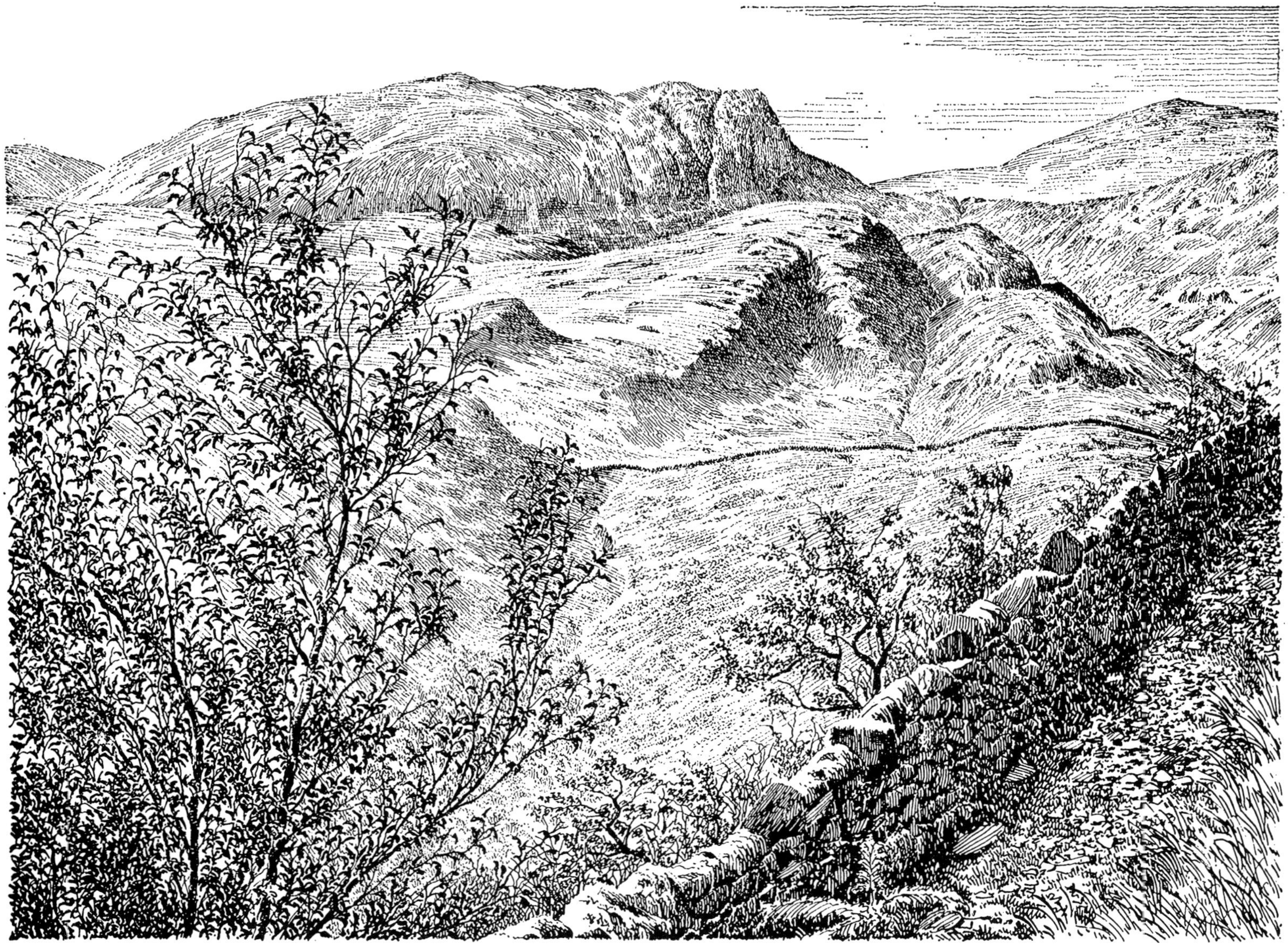

DOVE CRAG
There is unsuspected interest and charm in many of the smaller side-valleys of Lakeland and none rewards a leisurely exploration more than beautiful Dovedale, uninhabited and out of the sight and sound of Patterdale's busy traffic. Hazel woods lead up to a tangle of wild country where massive vegetation-capped boulders lie in chaotic confusion below the overhanging cliff of Dove Crag, inaccessible to all but the most expert of rock climbers.

S

S

S

LANGDALE PIKES, FROM SIDE PIKE

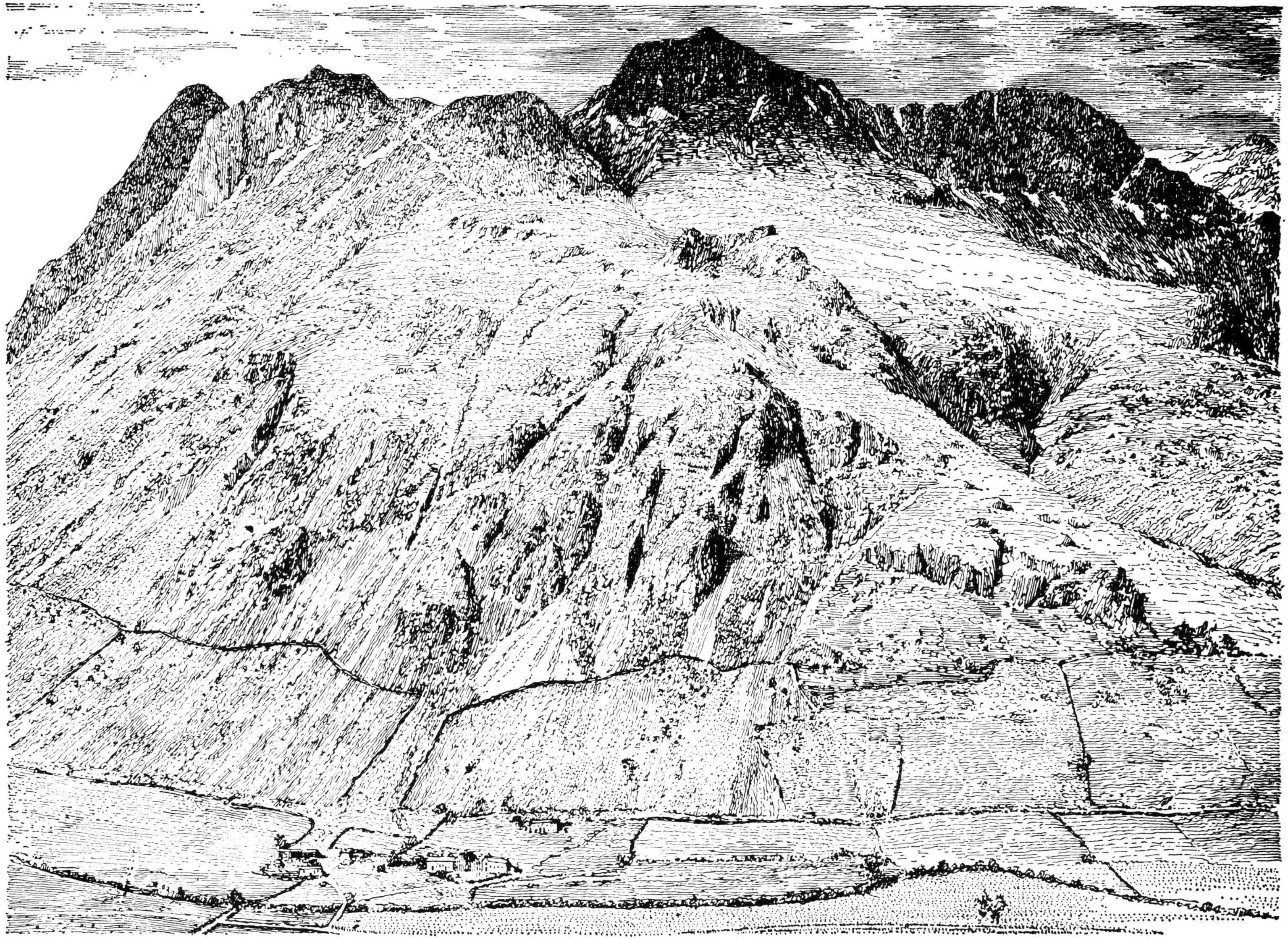

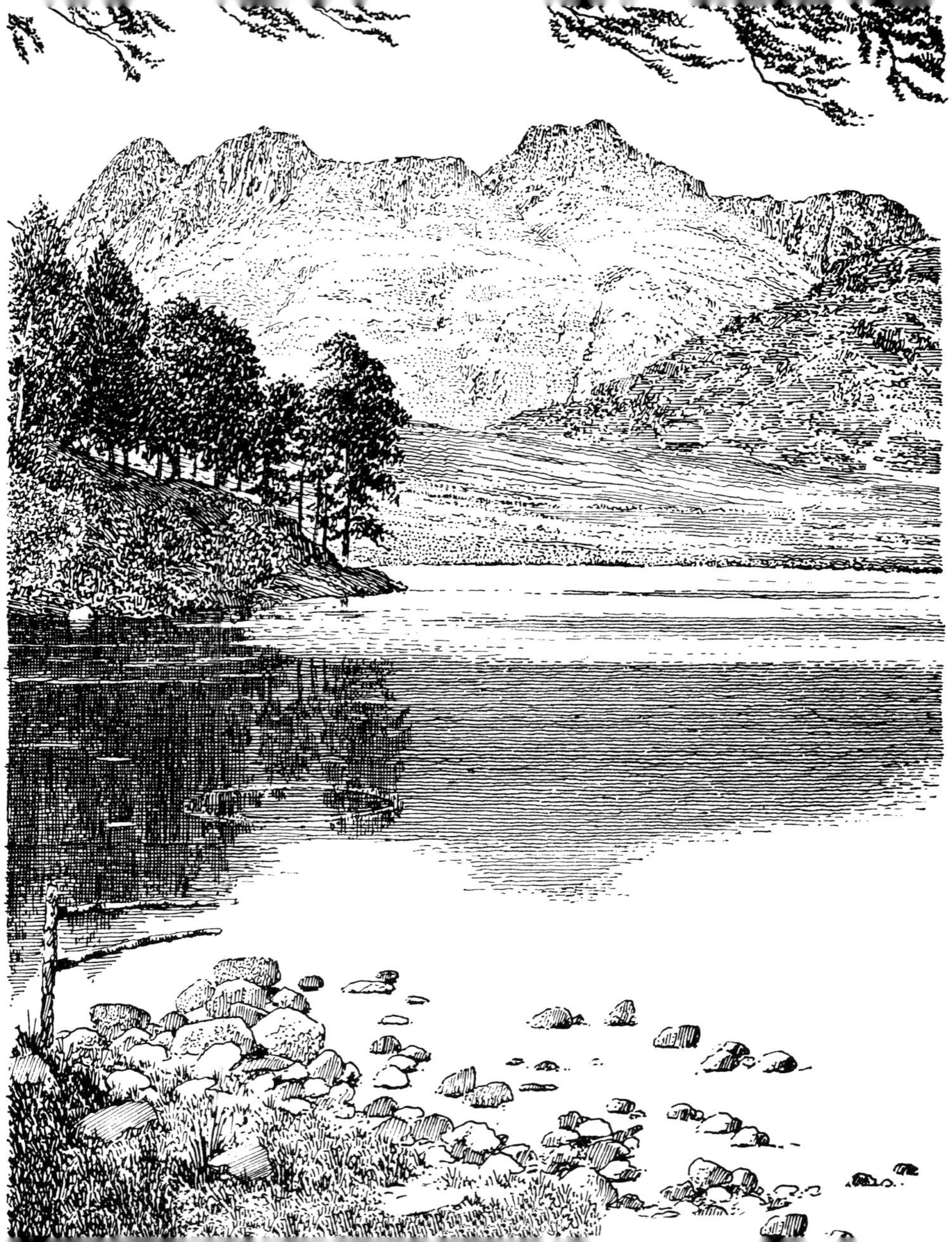

BLEA TARN

The Blea Tarn that all tourists know (there are others of the same name) occupies a hollow on the neck of high ground linking Great and Little Langdale, and, with its fringe of pines and rhododendrons, makes a perfect foreground to the dramatic backcloth of the Pikes as a century of artists, first with brush and latterly with camera, have told in pictures.

T

CANISP
Canisp is a bold pyramid of sandstone yet fails to compete in shapeliness with the surrounding mountains of Assynt. It has the misfortune to be a near neighbour of Suilven and is invariably seen in the latter's company; and if Suilven appears in a view nothing else gets much attention. Canisp is the only mountain hereabouts that looks ordinary and capable of ascent by normal fellwalking – which is, perhaps, a merit.

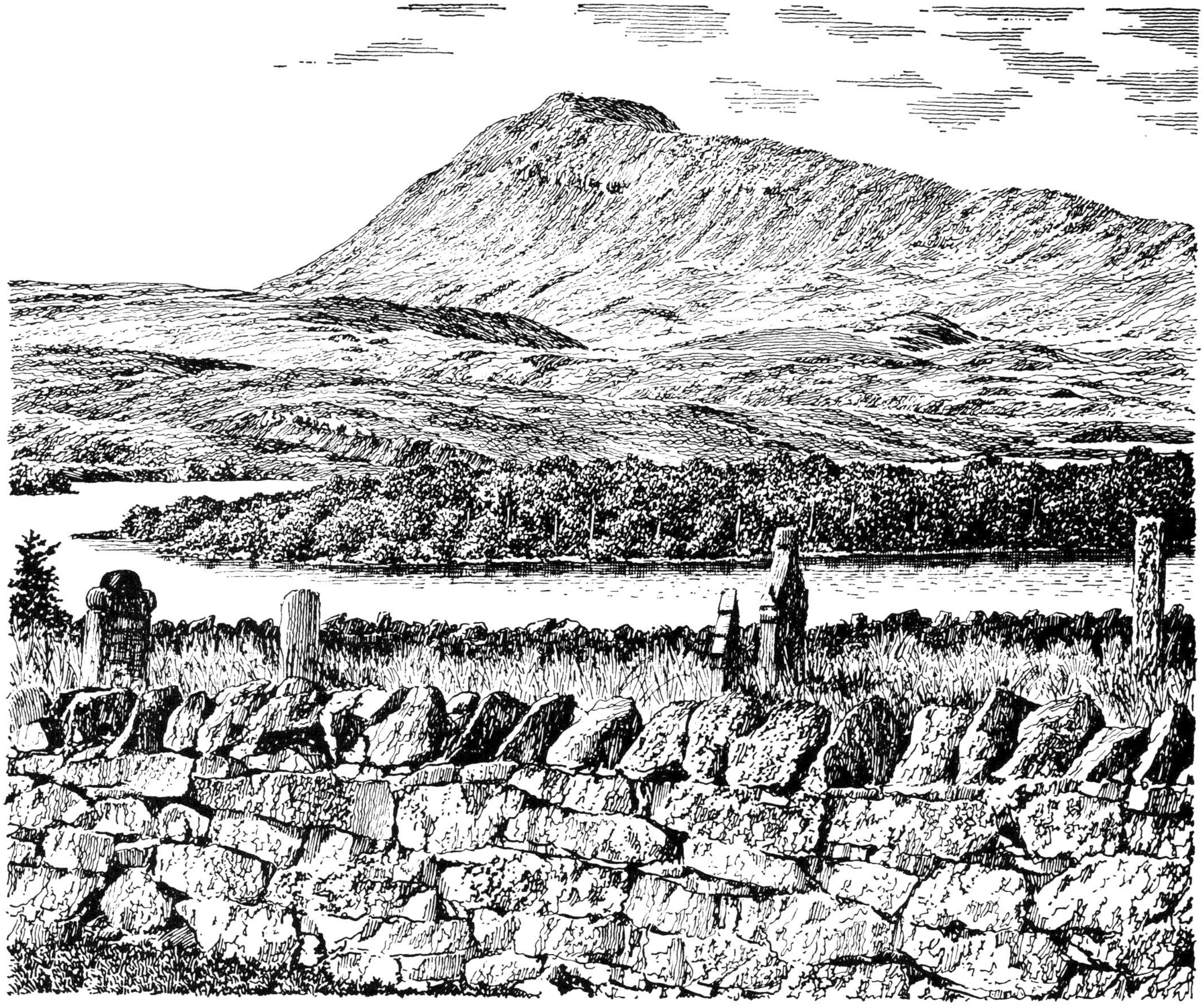

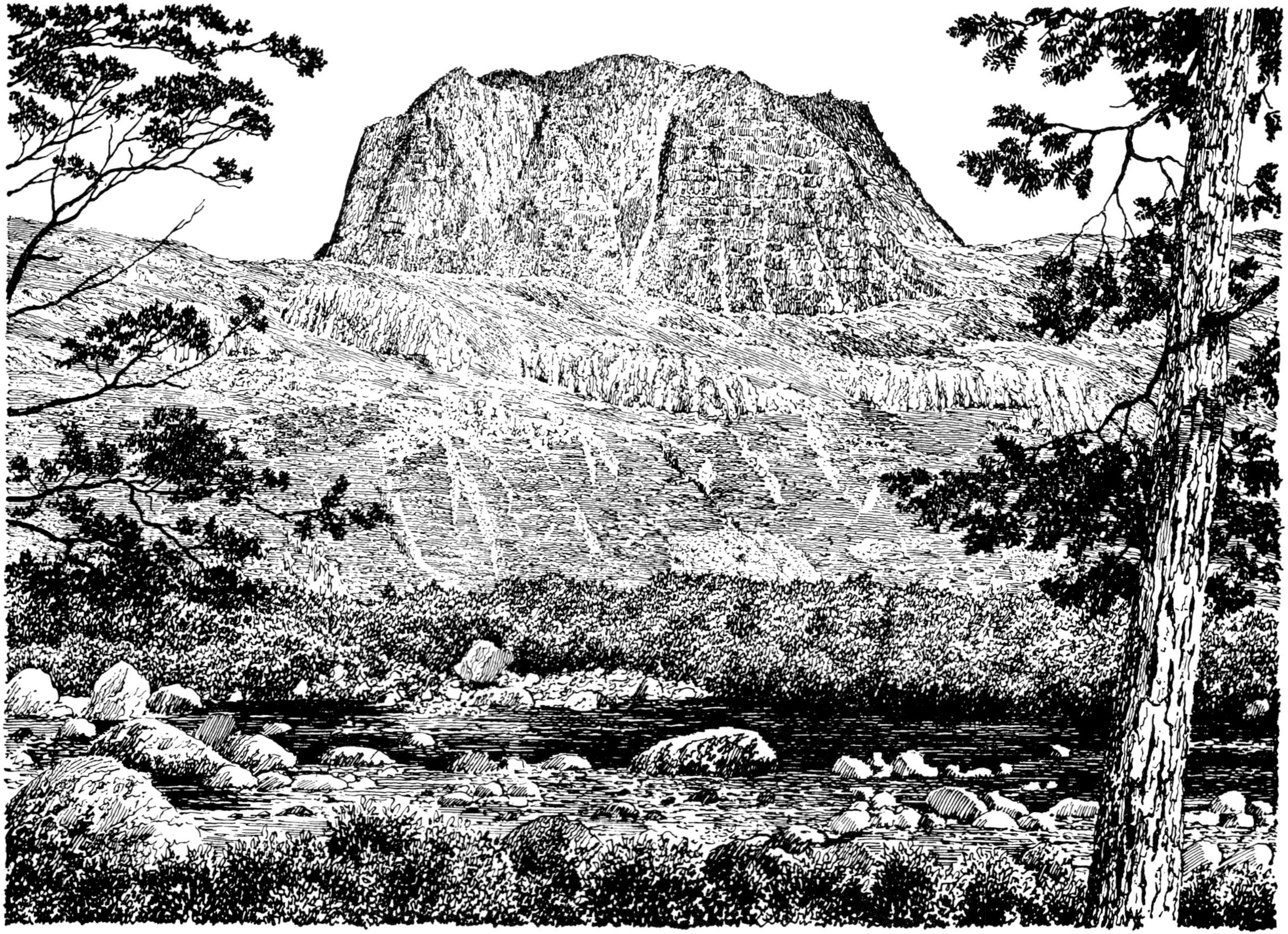

SLIOCH
When Slioch is seen across Loch Maree through the pines of Grudie it is posed perfectly, begging to be photographed. From here its steep buttresses and rocky tower seem impregnable, like a castle in the sky. Legions of passers-by have obliged.

U V

TRYFAN, FROM OGWEN
The rocky peak of Tryfan, towering into the sky above the Ogwen valley, is the most challenging of Snowdonia's mountains and its striking outline is the most admired. It also has the roughest terrain, the top in particular being a huge pile of boulders, difficult to negotiate and bounded by precipitous cliffs. Tryfan takes swift revenge on those who do not treat it with respect. But its ascent is an experience that lives long, and happily, in the memory.

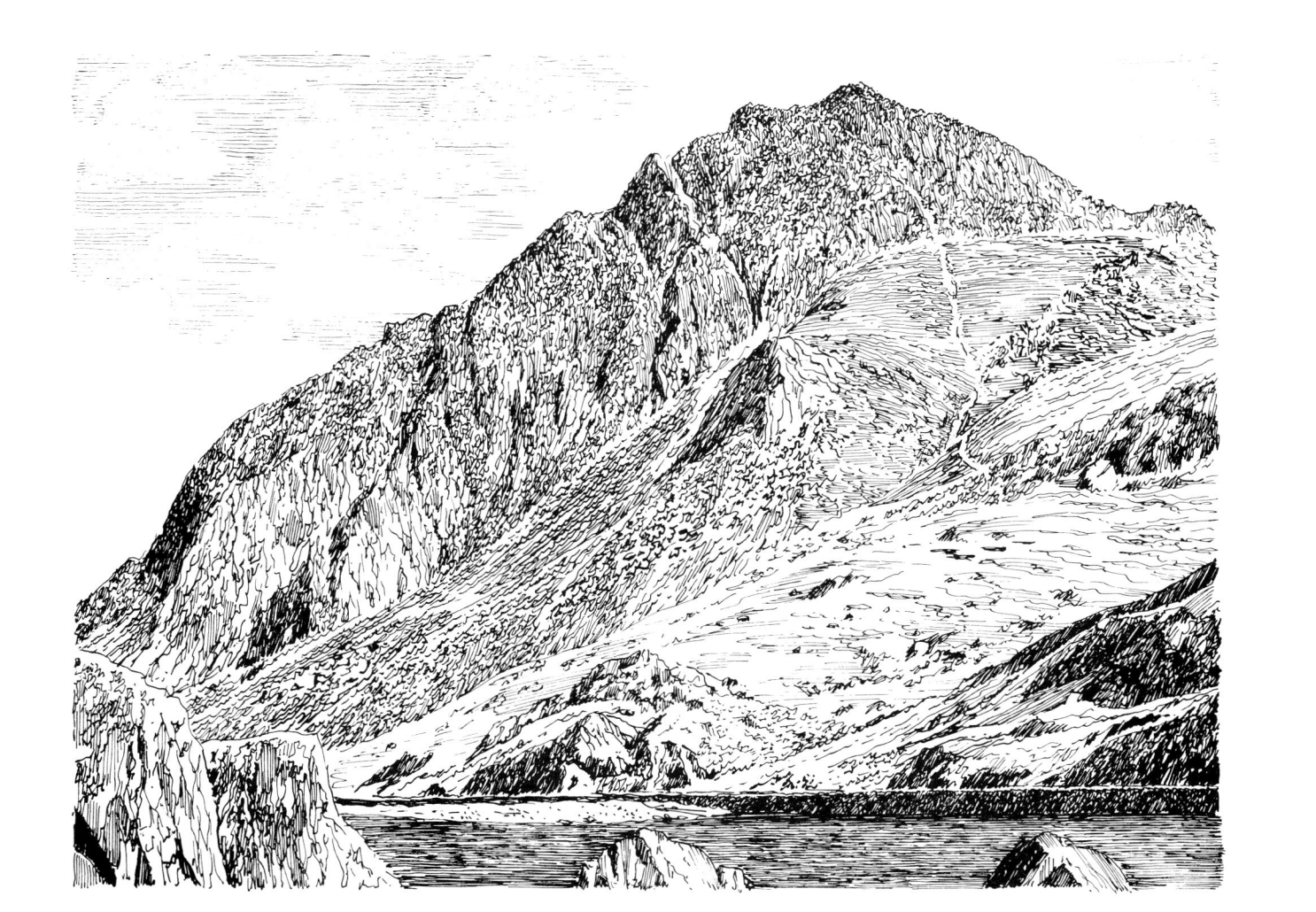

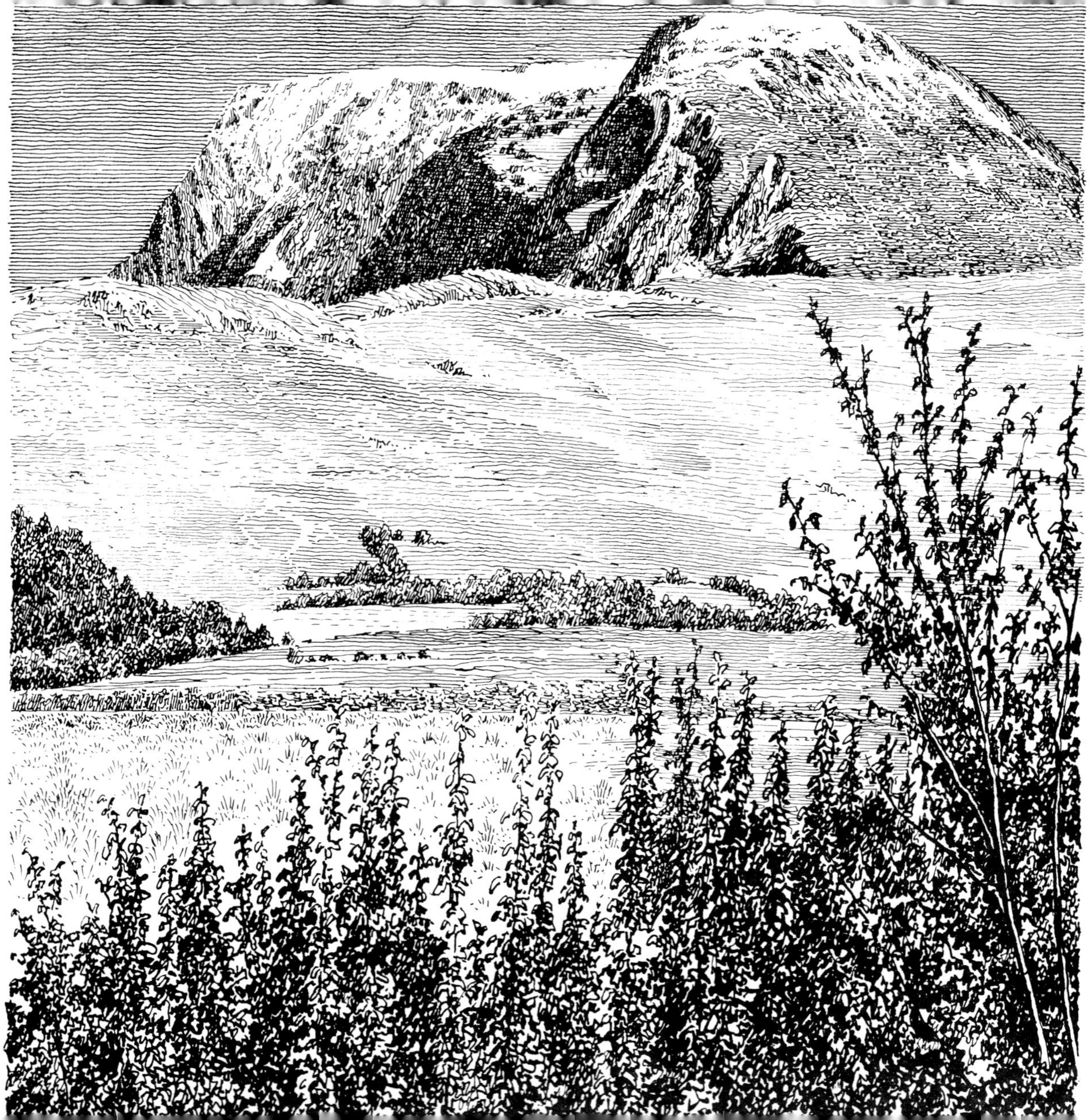

BEN NEVIS, FROM TORLUNDY

The most-favoured viewpoint for photographs of Ben Nevis is Corpach, perhaps because of the interesting foreground offered by the quaint buildings on the pier or by the war memorial, but it is not wholly satisfactory because the view includes only the merest suggestion of the great north-eastern cliffs that give the mountain its principle distinction. Moving eastwards from Fort William, these cliffs come splendidly into sight at Torlundy. Although partly obscured by intervening foothills, enough is seen of them to give an appreciation of their splendid architecture.

W

THE ROAD TO WATENDLATH

The most enchanting and romantic of all Lakeland's roads is the narrow byway leaving Borrowdale at Ashness Gate and ending at Watendlath, four miles away in a fold of the hills. If any Lakeland road should be closed for pleasure motoring it is this; but, instead, it has suffered many 'improvements' and the passage of cars has been smoothed and made easier by parking places, the result being summer congestion. Walkers have been diverted to a new footpath to save their skins. The squirrels have fled. There is noise where there was peace and quiet . . .

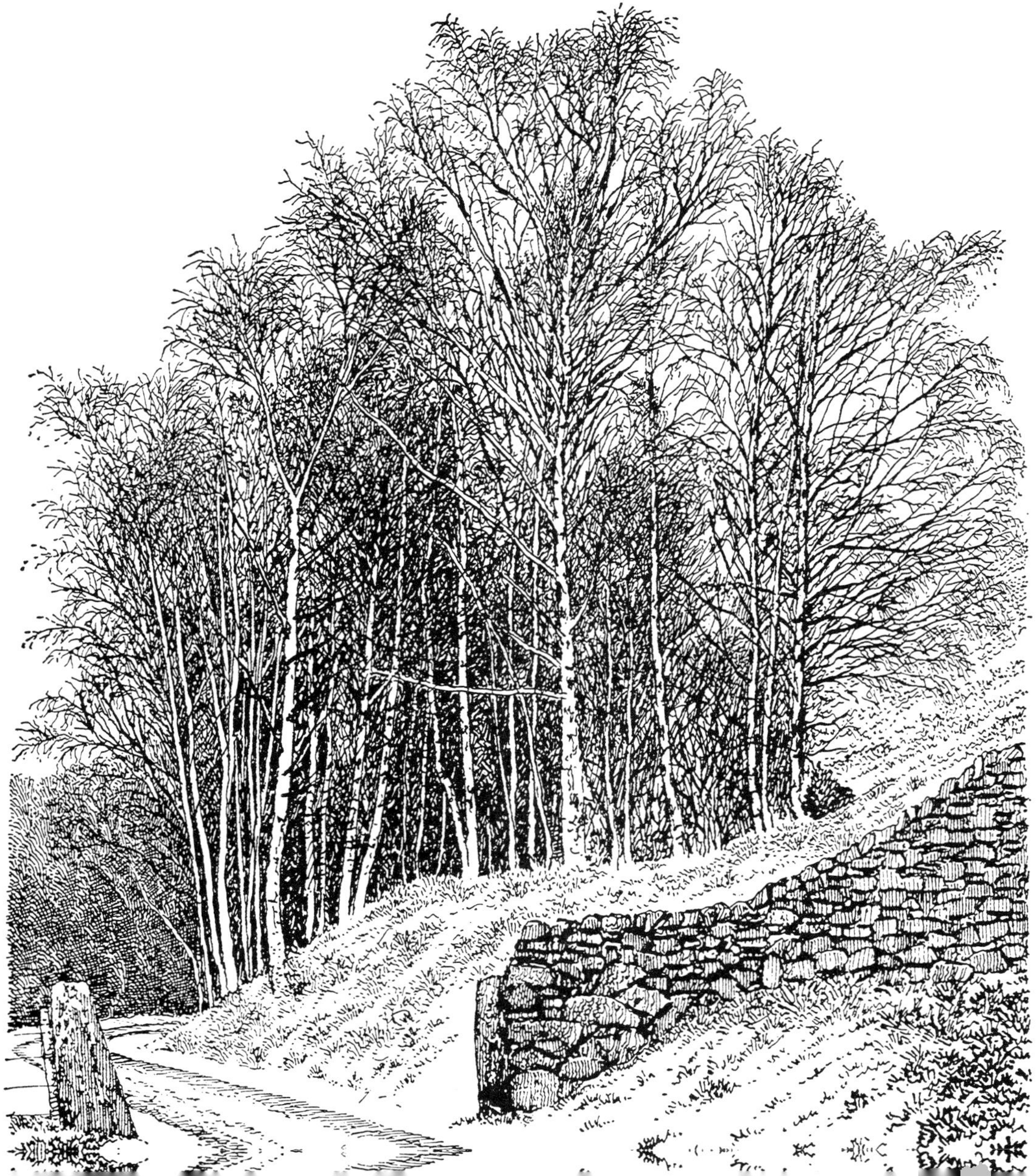

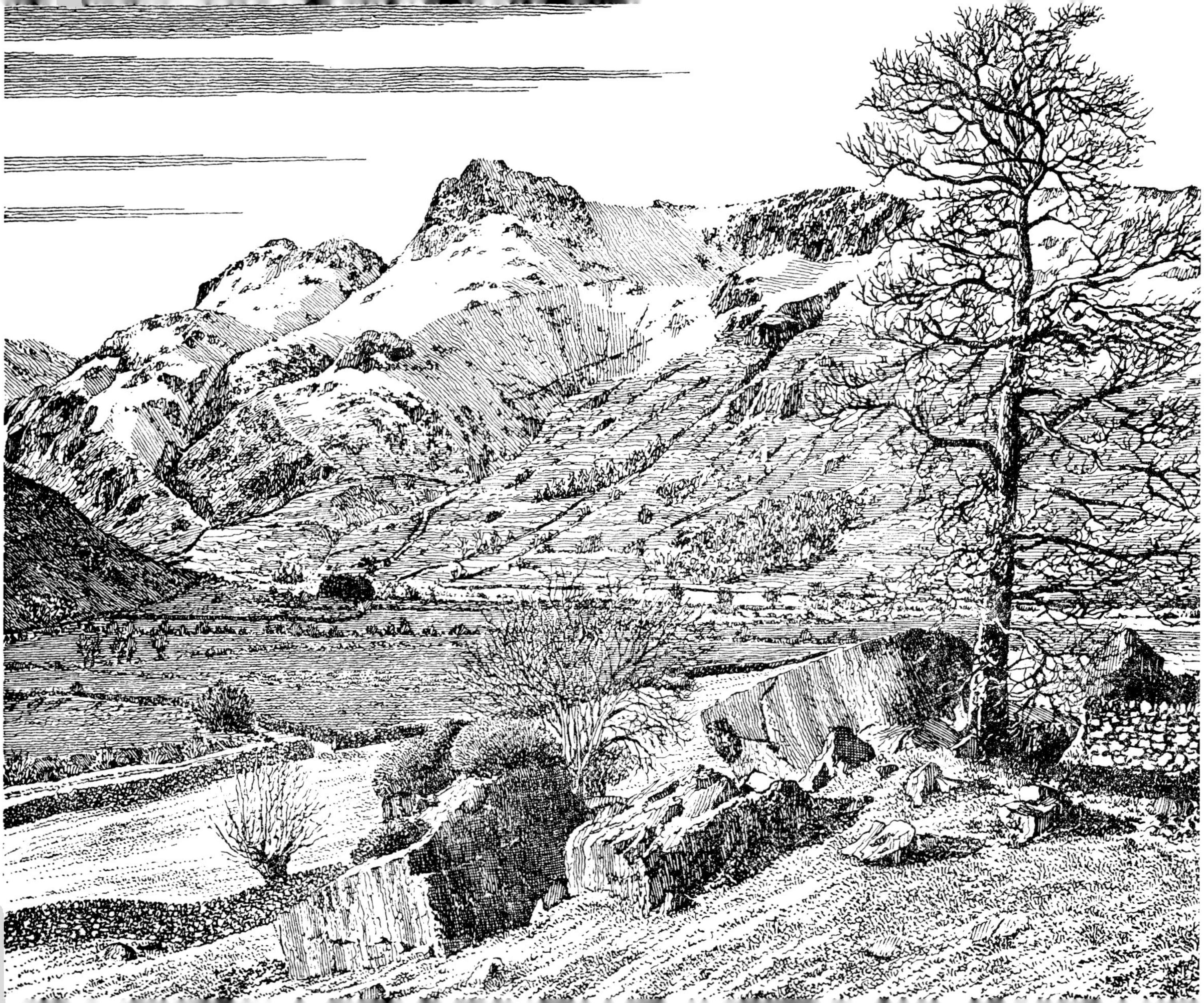

XYZ

LANGDALE PIKES, FROM CHAPEL STILE

XYZ